The Winds of Change

Praise for
The Winds of Change

"I've watched Julie Shannon walk through the kinds of storms that throttle many of us until we shrivel up, turn bitter, and give up on God and others. Remarkably, she's weathered these tempests and emerged full of life, love, and adventure. Within these pages, she describes her journey and offers insights to help you, a friend, or a loved one reframe these setbacks and emerge ready to move forward undaunted. Honest, personal, wise, and an enjoyable read, *Winds of Change* serves up cool drinks of refreshing spring water to weary travelers thirsty for the nourishment needed to overcome life's disappointments."

— **Sue Edwards**, DMin, Professor of Educational Ministries and Leadership, Dallas Theological Seminary, Author, *Discover Together Bible Study Series* and co-author of *40 Questions About Women in Ministry*

"Dr. Julie Shannon's book is a map for anyone who is down, drifting, or feeling defeated by the storms of life. Through practical tips and engaging stories, Julie guides the reader *through* the storm and reveals practical ways for an individual to focus on the future instead of the past."

— **Joseph Bojang**, MHR

"Julie writes as someone who has been there and has experienced storms up close and personal. As a cancer survivor, *Winds of Change* resonates . . . the shock of an unexpected diagnosis, the confusion because I felt I did everything right, and struggling to find a way forward. *Winds of Change* meets you where you are and gently provides insight to move forward. If you are alive, you will likely experience trauma or storms a few times in life . . . this book is a valuable resource to keep you from getting stuck and walk alongside others who are in the midst of a storm."

— **Sharyn King,** GFI, CIFT, CETI,
Operations Director, Powered to Move

"I picked up this book in the midst of my own storm and found comfort. Julie beautifully reveals her own story as she reminds us to trust God even in the pain and uncertainty. This book has joined my Bible and journal as I reflect on the storm, listen to my Heavenly Father, and choose to respond in hope."

— **Michelle Attar,** Pastor of Adult Ministries,
Bent Tree Bible Fellowship

"As a family law attorney of twenty-seven years, I have witnessed firsthand the kinds of storms that bring chaos and pain to people's lives. Julie offers an 'inside look' and guides you with steps to take in order to enhance healthy communication and personal development. I will definitely recommend this book to clients!"

— **Melinda Eitzen,** Founding Partner, Duffee + Eitzen

"Dr. Julie Shannon writes with raw emotion and authenticity about her journey through life's heavy disappointments: loss, infertility, divorce, and even natural disasters. Her encouragement toward honest self-reflection and a strong group of valued friends is a needed reminder. Through it all, Julie has found the value of reframing her losses and, most importantly, holding on to her strong faith in God. I would recommend this book to all who are on a mission of self-discovery after life throws them painful speed bumps."

— **Ann Marlowe Golding,** BS Edu, MABS

"Julie tells not only her story but also all of our stories in *The Winds of Change*. Her insights on weathering life's storms are direct and hope-filled. Julie provides practical help rooted in real-life experiences and shaped by biblical wisdom. If you are looking for concrete steps to prepare for real life, follow Julie's coaching through this book."

— **Neil Tomba,** Senior Pastor, Northwest Bible Church,
Author, *The Listening Road: One Man's Ride
Across America to Start Conversations About God*

"Julie is one of the most passionate and determined women I know. I am so encouraged every time I speak with her and learn of all her experiences on this journey of life. She has learned to navigate the stormy waters with grace and perseverance, which gives her an incredible insight into the waters that others are swimming in during the storms of life. Julie has been a friend to me during some very difficult times, and today, it is a great joy to see her helping so many on their journey of healing. I would recommend this book to anyone who needs to know that they are not alone. There is hope if we do not give up."

— **Peggy Banks,** DMin, CPLC, TICC

"Julie Shannon is the real deal, and her authenticity offers a warmth and thoughtfulness that reaches out through her writing to us, her readers. No matter where you find yourself on your life journey—walking through a storm, defining yourself to meet future storms, or facing an exciting life change—enter into these pages and allow Julie's voice, stories, and helpful guidance to transform your life in a positive, life-giving way."

— **Jodie Slater Hastings,** Cofounder, The Slate

"In her fascinating story-telling style, Dr. Shannon tells her story, and in so doing, she helps you make progress in your own story. Through compassionate transparency, she shares firsthand the trauma of riding out storms with knowledge gained by experience as well as professional training to help others who might be stuck. Whether you find yourself in the role of compassionate observer wishing you knew how to support someone dear to you or in a season of conflicted suffering because your world has been rocked by a storm, Julie will unwrap confusion and provide tools to help you offer practical compassion and find a way forward."

— **Willie O. Peterson,** DMin, MIDSOUTH Conference Assistant to Superintendent, Evangelical Covenant Church, Adjunct Professor, Doctor of Ministry Studies, Dallas Theological Seminary

"Change and trials are guaranteed in life. With wisdom and authenticity, Julie Shannon walks us through practical ways we can prepare for and cope with our own storms. I have personally benefitted from Julie's candor and insight in my life. You'll finish this book feeling like you had coffee with a big sister or a best friend, inspired by how Julie has leaned in with desperate dependence on Jesus."

— **Angela Cirocco,** Group Life Minister,
Northwest Bible Church

"Storms in life are inevitable. And yet, we often find ourselves unprepared for those tumultuous situations that cause us to lose our footing. Weaving in her own personal experiences (including that of being caught in a literal tornado!), Julie Shannon provides a path forward to help readers reframe and rebuild after life's blows, enabling us to embrace all seasons with authenticity and hope. *The Winds of Change* will inspire you to know yourself better, build up your community, and weather life's storms with purpose and courage."

— **M. Michelle Pokorny,** DMin,
Adjunct Professor of Doctor of Ministry Studies,
Dallas Theological Seminary

the Winds of Change

Defining Steps to
Build a Strong Foundation
& Weather Life Storms

JULIE SHANNON

NEW YORK

LONDON • NASHVILLE • MELBOURNE • VANCOUVER

The Winds of Change

Defining Steps to Build a Strong Foundation and Weather Life Storms

Published in New York, New York, by Morgan James Publishing. Morgan James is a trademark of Morgan James, LLC. www.MorganJamesPublishing.com

Proudly distributed by Ingram Publisher Services.

Scripture quotations taken from the (NASB®) New American Standard Bible®, Copyright © 1960, 1971, 1977, 1995 by The Lockman Foundation. Used by permission. All rights reserved. www.lockman.org.

A **FREE** ebook edition is available for you or a friend with the purchase of this print book.

CLEARLY SIGN YOUR NAME ABOVE

Instructions to claim your free ebook edition:
1. Visit MorganJamesBOGO.com
2. Sign your name CLEARLY in the space above
3. Complete the form and submit a photo of this entire page
4. You or your friend can download the ebook to your preferred device

ISBN 9781631959578 paperback
ISBN 9781631959585 ebook
Library of Congress Control Number: 2022936655

Cover Design by:
Megan Dillon
megan@creativeninjadesigns.com

Interior Design by:
Christopher Kirk
www.GFSstudio.com

Morgan James is a proud partner of Habitat for Humanity Peninsula and Greater Williamsburg. Partners in building since 2006.

Get involved today! Visit MorganJamesPublishing.com/giving-back

For those who've walked me through extraordinary life events.

Contents

Foreword

*B*efore retiring, I spent over forty years in the private practice of psychotherapy. Of course, I had office staff who helped my work run smoothly, and when I would discuss my telephone protocol with a new administrative assistant, I would remind that person: "Hardly anyone calls us to describe how terrific their life is, so prepare yourself. You're going to hear what emotional pain sounds like." Inevitably, it would take no time at all for the assistant to speak with me, wide-eyed, saying something like: "You weren't kidding! I had no idea how many different ways people can hurt!"

Each person, like it or not, is vulnerable to stormy interludes in life. None of us makes it to the finish line with a perfect flow of bright and cheery circumstances. So, just as I instructed my staff, I readied myself each day to walk individuals through the process of figuring it all out. Indeed, it was a privilege to become an insider with people in the midst of personal strains.

Once a new client came to my office, I would take as much background information as possible, and then, before finishing our first session, I'd ask: "What do you hope to accomplish by coming here?" It was a simple question, yet not really. First, my framing of the question put the person on notice that he or she could and would take the lead in the change process. I could be helpful, but it was ultimately that person's responsibility. Second, it would be one of many times I would keep that individual focused on the end result. We both knew that something needed to be different, but what? And that something had a way of revealing itself, then morphing as the weeks and months passed. Many loaded topics would come to the fore in our discussions, and as we dissected them, those clients felt both heard and relieved.

As Julie Shannon clearly teaches in this book, no one is exempt from the storms life brings. This being a broken world and each person being flawed, it should surprise no one that something outside our neatly scripted agenda is going to go wrong. It is unavoidable. As a therapist, I understood that and worked to provide a safe space for hope and confidence to emerge as shaken individuals sifted through their peculiar circumstances. I believed then, as I continue to believe now, that change can happen. But to get there, we needed a map, a plan.

As I would get to know my clients, I knew our work would be enhanced if I could bring in other resources, especially books, that would keep the focus clear. Being a writer and reader myself, I had become familiar with plenty of authors who would spur readers toward necessary inside-out adjustments. I would feel special relief when my clients locked in with a writer who could frame what the change process is all about. Julie Shannon is one such writer.

She shows an uncanny knack for identifying with her audience in an engaging, empathic manner. As you read, you will quickly discover that she is one who gets it. She gives words to the broad array of emotions and confusions associated with unwanted setbacks, then tenderly walks with you, blending pertinent psychological and spiritual insights with pragmatic directives.

No one wants to feel alone in the process of sifting out the stormy segments of life, and as you glean from Julie's personal insights and wisdom, you will conclude, as I did, that others have survived traumas and you can too. The change process can initially seem daunting, but once you learn to apply the right tools, that process can truly be transformative. May God's peace be with you as you learn from this special guide.

Les Carter, Ph.D.

Introduction

Several years ago, a mentor, Vickie Kraft, asked me a question that forever changed my life: "Are you taking steps toward your destination?"

This simple question stopped me in my tracks. I confess I sometimes focus too much on the present (especially when trying to survive some very difficult situations) and neglect to dedicate the time to look at what I need, and want, to move forward into the future.

I've faced a lot of storms (both literally and figuratively), and I knew God's presence in the midst of them. I'm a Christ-follower, and my personal experience has proven God's tender watch over me.

But now, when I look back on my life, I see how God used challenging seasons to send me in a new direction. I believe that God is good and does not cause bad things to happen but uses all things for our good and his glory. When everything seems uncertain, God often lays out a brand-new path.

As an example of God's faithfulness in directing me, three huge life storms—infertility, childlessness, and divorce—led to mentoring, speaker training, graduate school, and years of being a public speaker and writer.

Your situation, whatever it is, will look different. Every storm or change in life we face is unique to us. However, each circumstance offers a common opportunity for growth and connection, especially when we walk in community together.

With God's help, we can find our footing in the middle of uncertain, fearful, and extraordinary times. We can discover and grow in our intention and gain the tools to rebuild, remodel, and reframe our journey.

And please understand, this book is not intended to be a cry of fear and sadness but a calm voice of encouragement in the face of life's realities.

In the pages ahead, we will look at real examples of how people overcame the unexpected and summoned the courage to move through life storms. Beyond these stories we find practical, definitive steps to build the foundation we need to confidently stand strong during our turbulent moments.

And don't worry—even if we get off the path or take a couple of steps backward, we can choose to reevaluate and reengage. We continue with our forward momentum as we set our sights on our desired destination.

We all know that life is a marathon, not a sprint. If you stand in a place right now—in the middle of grief, divorce, financial or personal loss, confusion about what the future holds—know that you are not alone.

Consider this book a guide as you pursue your adventure. I'm sharing personal experiences, along with stories and conversations with others, so you can learn practical and empathetic ways to not only walk out your own journey but also come alongside others in theirs.

God created us for community, so let's walk together and explore different ways to cope with the chaos, wind our way through the curves of doubt, climb the mountains of challenging rubble, and overcome devastation to make our time here on Earth count for good.

One point of clarity: When I encourage others to explore their God-created selves and surroundings, I in no way mean that you should abandon a covenant, commitment, or promise. Only in life-altering and dangerous situations should this be considered and then involve the appropriate professionals to help. When we have a family commitment, marital covenant, friendship bond, community pledge, or church responsibilities, we ought to pursue every means possible to work out and reconcile the relationship and situation. Please seek out the appropriate guidance with this if needed.

So, let me ask a version of the question my mentor asked me: *Are the steps you are taking leading to your desired destination?*

As we journey together, we'll talk about:

- Who are we as uniquely created individuals?
- What kind of people do we want to be?
- What is our desired destination? (How do we see it right now, and how can we stay flexible for future adjustments to the plan?)
- How do we find joy and hold onto contentment, compassion, and hope?
- In what ways can we engage with community, family, friends, co-workers, neighbors, social media?

(Answer these now and then see how your answers might change through this time together.)

No matter where you are on your faith journey, I hope you will use these answers to assist you in whatever beliefs you hold dear.

When the winds of change blow in unexpected challenges of life, remember that you were created for this time and place. I've been there, and I'm cheering you on!

Thanks for joining me. Let's go!

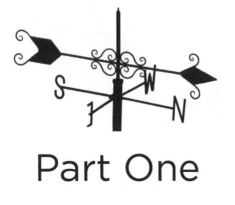

Part One

Storms

Chapter One

Surviving the Storm

*"And the rain fell, and the floods came, and the winds
blew and slammed against that house; and yet it
did not fall, for it had been founded on the rock."*
— Matthew 7:25

The violent storm roared over and around the house, leaving behind an eerie silence. After the walls stopped shaking, I fumbled for the doorknob, turned it, and stepped into the hallway to assess the damage.

Tornadoes in Texas were not uncommon, and I grew up with an underlying, unhealthy fear of them, but never in a million years did I believe I'd actually ride through one.

I grabbed a flashlight from the backpack I had with me in the bathroom "safe space" and peered around the doorframe, not sure if I would see a solid ceiling or starlight when I looked up (the electricity went out just before the tornado hit the house). In the surrounding thick darkness, there was an overwhelming smell of chlorophyll. Tiny particles of leaves, dust, and insulation were suspended in the narrow beam of light. I'd never smelled anything like that before—it was a smothering odor like a hundred freshly mowed lawns compressed into the living space of a house.

The first room checked out: ceiling in place, walls and windows intact (although I had no way of knowing the condition of the roof).

The interior of the house seemed relatively unscathed until I reached the last room.

Broken glass lay scattered across the bed, and tree branches were strewn everywhere. Leaves, shredded pink insulation, and broken slate projectiles appeared like the confetti aftermath of an outrageous party. Broken window shades lifted and slapped as the breeze blew through the shards of glass still clinging to the window frames.

Though much of the room reflected the storm's violence, not one picture frame on the wall seemed disturbed . . . they were all perfectly aligned in the unsettled calm.

During its dark of night descent, the monster ripped a multi-mile path across the heart of the city. Immediately after the impact, a strange, lengthy pause hovered above before the chaotic screams of sirens began.

People up and down the street yelled through windows to confirm survival and determine injury. Many of us couldn't leave our homes because trees had been tossed like twigs and lay haphazardly across sidewalks and rooftops. Power lines were down and dangerous debris added to the post-storm mess.

An hour later, multiple flashlights came bobbing down the street and loud voices urgently called for evacuation. Police and fire first responders put their lives in danger to walk in to save those now threatened by a gas leak in the storm's aftermath.

The next few hours revealed real-life tales of heroes, heroines, miraculous rescues, and harrowing escapes. The tornado proved historic and caused an unwelcome two-year-plus journey of reframing and rebuilding.

The tornado only added insult to injury.

For me, this unsettling time heaped more than physical debris. After chronic issues with infertility, an unwelcome divorce (finalized the year prior to the tornado), and an uncertain future, I knew the natural disaster only added to a personal, internal storm.

All of these events proved intense but little did I know there was more to come.

I remember my exact location when I got "the call." I was sitting in my home office when my cell phone rang and I saw the number of a former relative.

When I answered, she told me that my ex-husband had died from COVID-19 complications. I sat stunned and sad. To be honest, I felt a complicated mix of emotions.

From the outside, our almost seventeen-year marriage looked to the world like we had it all. He was an attorney, we resided in lovely homes, and we were involved in church activities. Both of us served our church community in a variety of ways: teaching Bible studies, serving on committees, and numerous leadership aspects of our Sunday school class.

But we all know looks can be deceiving.

For years, I had wanted (and tried) to make my life and my marriage fit the image we projected to the outside world. I suspect even now there may be a few people who will be surprised and maybe even a little shocked to learn some of the behind-the-scenes reality of what was going on in my life.

The reason I am willing to "pull back the curtain" is because I found that the storm of a rocky marriage (and one that ends in divorce) offers many opportunities for hiding, isolation, defeat, humiliation, self-doubt, criticism, and lots of raw pain. (Sadly, in the church world, the fear of being judged by others often leads the list.)

Even now, I find myself fighting through the fear of revealing too much about my situation. But in order to let you know I can truly relate to unexpected life realities, I need to peel back a few layers and remove any ambiguous references of what happened to me. Just a generic referral to "a divorce" probably won't help anyone who might sit in a similar experience.

I want to let you in on my story of divorce and other hard challenges in hopes that if someone finds themselves in a similar situation, they can gain encouragement from what I have learned, not only from my experiences but also from the stories of others.

That said, I have found that the church can be a place where difficult trials live in silence and are, at times, even shunned to a banished land.

You see, I always knew and believed that "with God all things were possible" (see Matthew 19:26). But there also seemed to be an unspoken expectation that if you truly "walk with the Lord," then even the worst of situations *should* work out.

You just need to trust enough, try hard enough, and play by the rules.

But life, at least for me, wasn't always neat and tidy underneath. I (for whatever reason) never felt like I could expose what was really going on except to a very close inner circle of friends, a few family members, a therapist, and a mentor.

I spent a lot of my life really wanting to please everyone. But people-pleasing can also lead to shame and embarrassment, especially when you feel like it's unacceptable to look like you don't have it all together.

Sometimes we believe the lie that if we have the appearance of living our best life, it somehow makes the gospel more "attractive" or can make us feel worthy of the Christian label. When really, we're *all* sinners saved by grace through faith.

For me, private reality always seemed at war with public vulnerability.

Still, I always strived to do the right things.

When it came to our marital issues, although I truly believe it wasn't the primary cause, we walked through a heartbreaking struggle with infertility. I was fortunate to be in a church community that gave me great support through that difficult journey.

Years of infertility treatments and three miscarriages later, I realized that biological motherhood would remain an unfulfilled dream, and unfortunately, we weren't in agreement about adoption.

Sadly, after many years of working on my marriage (with professional therapists, close friends, Bible study and ministry leaders, and Christian mentors), we finally came to the end of the road.

God's Word, woven throughout my life, sustained me then as it does now. Yet I found myself faced with the fallout of two really difficult issues in the church: infertility and divorce.

I share these details with you so you'll know I've been through some severe storms and I've walked a few very dark paths. I've known fear, uncertainty, and many other emotions. Yet through it all, I've also known the lovingkindness and presence of God with me, no matter what. That doesn't mean things were easy or I didn't have times of doubt or anger at God, but I learned to trust him and rely on him *through it all*.

When I think about great winds of life blowing, I think of trees that sway and bend in the gusts and gales. There exists push and pull—give and take. The tree sways, but it can also snap. Eventually, the incessant winds broke that marriage tree for me.

But here's the good news: God can take all our storms and transform them for good.

Maybe you need to know you're not alone or that someone else walked through a hellish situation for a very long time, clinging to hope, one step at a time. Life is a journey, and none of us knows what will come next, but we have an Almighty Creator and Savior who loves and leads us. By his grace, we feel his care in the midst of the gusting winds and the torrential storms.

I've worked through a lot in order to gain a new perspective of joy and hope for the future. God's forgiveness and release give me a freedom that nothing else can.

After the tornado, I watched the reframing of houses that had too much damage for minor repairs. Fresh two-by-fours set a stronger structure for the recovered dwelling place. This kind of physical rebuilding offers a good visual for what we need to do after life storms do their damage.

I have learned "reframing" can refer to a different way to consider something. Often, we decide to change the frame of a picture to enhance it and bring new life. Reframing helps us consider a variety of ways to look at our lives: where we are, how to repair collateral damage, ways we might engage in looking at our circumstances from a different angle.

Let's define our direction through the winds of change and move forward knowing that endings bring new beginnings, that the sun rises after the dark storms of night. No matter where we find ourselves, we always have hope for a brighter tomorrow.

Chapter Two

Reframing in the Aftermath

*O*ne day I was crying to my therapist and said, "I feel like I'm holding my dogs and standing in the rubble and ashes of seventeen years of life. It's all gone or, at the very least, cast in a new understanding and reality. The world I built is lying in ruins at my feet."

I had fought for my marriage (with godly people helping me) for many, many years.

And yet . . . here I stood.

Having recently graduated from seminary, I anticipated my divorce would impact the future of my work. In the midst of this debilitating pity party, my therapist grabbed my attention.

"Yes, you could stand there looking at all that you've lost. Or, you might consider a different perspective. You *got* to have seventeen years of couple friends and community. You *got* to have incredible friends that truly lived the Christian life together. You *got* to have a house that you enjoyed. You *got* to have numerous relationships and experiences you wouldn't have otherwise," he said.

As an objective, professional therapist (and grounded person of Christian faith), he helped me reconsider and reframe a devastating time and start to restructure my thoughts, to begin climbing out of that negative pile of debris. I had not sought or desired the outcome of that period of life; however, I had the opportunity to learn great lessons, evaluate the time, turn in a new direction, and seek to follow God where he would lead.

Of course, I realized I had a choice. I could stand in the mess and grow bitter. Or I could choose to visualize the journey through a lens of hope and joy.

Don't get me wrong. This wasn't an overnight change of heart or sudden turn of events. But eventually, it became my mental default—to know I did the very best I could under the circumstances. I sought wise counsel, trusted God, and began to step forward in hope.

Begin Where You Are

Have you ever felt like the life you built crumbled down around you and needed a reset? Or faced a deep need for a major job change? Maybe something like whether or not to go to college or trade school, or even graduate school? Perhaps you need a new creative outlet and feel fearful of trying. Sometimes we have to make decisions about moving someplace new because of a job change or marriage or a great adventure!

Not long ago, I left my hometown and relocated to a new city.

The seed for this journey was planted many years before, and after it lay dormant through my many life changes, it finally sprouted. I watched God unfold events and open doors in extraordinary ways for me to pursue this new plan. So, I took a deep breath, said yes, packed my bags, and ventured into the unknown.

Almost everyone I told about my "big life change" responded with great excitement. I had several conversations with friends of different ages and in various stages of their own life decisions.

For some people, making a move like this might not be that big of a deal. For others, just the thought was overwhelming. I fell somewhere in between. I adore the new setting and have met wonderful people. To be honest, I relocated in the summer during the pandemic when most routines and events were limited or scattered. Finding ways to immediately get plugged into places and groups proved challenging. I experienced joyful moments and some lonely ones too.

I'm grateful for my community of friends and family who consistently checked in after I moved. Thankfully, I had writing projects and deadlines on which to focus, and that often challenged me!

I committed to get out in my non-work time and to explore: I found new sights, ate delicious food, enjoyed fun events, and met some delightful people.

But change isn't easy, even if it's welcome.

Once we reach that glorious stage of "adulting" (and some days, I confess I just want to throw on my "I'm done adulting, let's go to Disney World" T-shirt and go!), we are never too old or young to embrace new things, people, locations, and adventure. Sure, we all have our individual situations and preferences that can limit our choices. Seeking long-term life goals to stay open to new growth experiences often gives us the time and space to expand our world and step into different seasons, no matter our age.

As adults, we face opportunities to embrace joyful decisions or to experience moments that turn our lives upside down. We might discover a desire to simply tweak a few small things in life or, instead, to embrace huge differences.

Small or big, change can be unnerving, even scary, but I want to encourage you (and me) to face fear head-on and never let it win the day! When we see our dreams begin to unfold, let's step in!

The pandemic gave me the opportunity and space to publish my first book and also launch *The Bearing Life® Podcast* (more about this later). Then after a while, I watched, astounded, as God provided an unmistakable opportunity to relocate to a place I'd quietly dreamed of for years. I did some preparation work, took a deep breath, and, Indiana Jones-style,[1] took a step toward the unknown abyss and trusted that a path would unfold. I felt a solid conviction to "go," so I moved to a new place.

I had to choose faith over fear: stepping toward a new vision of vibrant life and taking the opportunity to pursue new skills, revisit past dreams, and begin to build a community.

My winds had changed.

Defining Ourselves in the Storm

Here's a question worth exploring. What can we, as imperfect people, do in order to truly live our lives to the fullest? How do we interact with the winds that blow in and blast us without warning?

Even when winds blow all around us, we have the choice in how we respond. If we run or walk away, the gusts might come along so swiftly that our steps can't keep up and we scramble to maintain a sense of stability and control.

Or maybe we can stand firm, "hunker down," and keep our back to the swirling disarray, allowing it to move on around us. We can also turn and face those gusts head-on with resolution, knowing the disasters we face. Maybe that force will hold us upright or give us the forward motion to get through to the other side.

As we all know, situations and extraordinary events can show up and unexpectedly assault us. When they hit, the whirlwind can knock us off balance or bring on action paralysis or a temporary inability to call upon rational thoughts or coping skills.

The unique events and effects of a once-in-a-lifetime world-wide pandemic caused great adjustment and change, and often painful loss. Maybe you found yourself reevaluating your life goals or job. Maybe you received a life-altering, middle-of-the-night phone call or text.

No matter who we are, where we live, what age or season we walk through right now, someday we will experience great loss.

We *don't* have a choice about certain disturbances in life—when or if they show up, what they look like, or the amount of damage they might cause. We *do* have a choice to determine who we are in the midst or aftermath.

Just as a literal gale brings chaos, life upheavals can cause emotional, physical, spiritual, and mental challenges. People often won't talk about them. They can retreat into unhealthy isolation at best, or worse, dive into dangerous self-medicating behaviors or self-harm tendencies. Ongoing feelings of aloneness multiply and affect our perspective and ability to even comprehend where to begin taking the small steps of rebuilding life or pursuing a new path.

Life storms create a world of disorder and confusion, depending on the nature of the challenge. The variety of disruptions can feel daunting, and no one holds immunity against them. We all travel through life holding on to hope and promise, never wanting adversity, confusion, or tough times.

The desire to try something new can cause stress as well. We might want to explore a hobby or respond to that deep-down yearning to create art.

These pursuits often require reframing life. Certainly not quite as deeply or catastrophically as a major trauma, they still often bring along a measure of fear, insecurity, and doubt about our ability to learn something new or to finally give ourselves permission to try that "one thing" we've never quite had the boldness to try.

People of faith know that we aren't promised an easy road; in fact, we read and learn in the Bible that we should *expect* troubles in this imperfect world. People who claim no faith innately know the realities of daily life and how every one of us will experience some form of difficulty in our earthly years.

One of my current favorite verses to find biblical encouragement is, "And the rain fell, and the floods came, and the winds blew and slammed against that house; and yet it did not fall, for it had been founded on the rock" (Matthew 7:25). My faith foundation rests on Jesus, and even though things can be difficult, painful, and scary, my eternal hope rests in him.

This verse reminds us to turn to him and *know* that when we can't grasp the whys or hows, we should just keep putting his living word before our eyes. We can continue to take it into our minds and hearts as a reminder of who he is even when we don't comprehend life.

Please hear me: During hard-to-understand events and circumstances, I've had moments of questioning God. I'm not suggesting that you run to this verse and just read it as "everything will be okay." In the midst of difficulty and confusion, we find the unexplainable or uncertainty hard to comprehend. Even those of us with strong, grounded faith find ourselves questioning.

What we draw from requires a shift in focus. We keep our eyes on Jesus and trust him in the middle of the storm. This doesn't mean we understand or don't feel pain or fear. We trust and have faith. We stand firm in the belief that our Almighty God lovingly holds all things together.

He is the steady post that the wind vane attaches to. No matter the direction or force of the storm, he IS.

Trust me, I know this can be really hard to remember in the midst of raw grief and suffering. When we can't summon the encouragement for ourselves, let's make sure we have others who kindly and empathetically remind us that we ultimately find our source and rest in him. Not as an easy fix to promote guilt when we aren't in that strong frame of mind yet, but as a gentle, hopeful reminder.

A Closer Look: The Winds of Trauma & Stress

Kaleidoscopes fascinate me. One slight turn transforms the internal pieces and parts into a variety of beautiful patterns and colors.

My guest Katlyn (Kat) joined me on the podcast to discuss trauma.[2] In our discussion of big "T" trauma and little "t" trauma, we even came up with an impromptu medium "t" trauma.

If we think about the different kinds of stress we carry within us, the broken pieces and patterns might be a slight internal irritant, or they could be really harsh, life-altering traumas that affect our everyday behaviors and worries, maybe without our knowing. By taking a closer look, we can see that some of our pieces require a lot of work, and some minor ones just need to be released.

Let's take time to figure out if they are traumatic, problematic, or just frustrations.

As Kat described, "Every human on Earth has some form of trauma in their life history."[3] Trauma can be a life-changing event, a tragic encounter, ongoing work stress, or a negative influencing voice from childhood that had a long-term impact. Depending on the nature of the trauma, it might affect our brains and bodies[4] in ways that engage us in constant fight or flight modes.

When we experience temporary stress, we take time to process our pain and include others for support as well. Whether we need to go to a specialist for gastro issues, a physical therapist, or a talk therapist, we must advocate for ourselves and involve others to help us understand what we are experiencing.

We might need a combination of people helping us work through specific issues or situations. "Take time and recognize how you feel. Avoiding your feelings won't help and could cause future issues. Understand that you are more than a body system. You are a whole person who is a collection of body systems. Fortunately, we have a lot of specialists available to us for the different systems."[5]

Kat encouraged us to honor the word *trauma*, to process, identify, and understand different situations in life. We need to make sure we don't ignore issues or over/underreact. A key question to ask ourselves: "Is it traumatic or problematic?"[6]

When we feel knots of stress pain in our muscles, or the burn of acid in our stomach, or an inability to focus or maybe a short-trigger temper, we invest our time wisely when we examine the big picture of the symptoms. We need to look beneath the surface and process the underlying issues. Learning more about the brain/body interaction, sorting out what needs to be addressed, and including the appropriate people (friends, family, and medical professionals) is important self-care and contributes to our overall health and joy.

Let's give ourselves the respect and dignity to pay attention and move through and process memories or emotions to ensure a healthier walk through life.

Chapter Three

Storm Preparation

*D*uring my third pregnancy, I hopefully anticipated a sonogram appointment.

After two previous miscarriages, I was thrilled to have made it far enough along to not only see the tiny little heartbeat but also to anticipate finally hearing one. I joyfully arrived for the milestone appointment, but several minutes after the exam began, the sonographer stopped talking. I could tell she was searching for something on the screen.

Suddenly, she stopped and told me to get dressed and go down the hall to meet with my doctor. Not understanding, I asked about listening to the heartbeat. Coldly, she turned her back on me, said there was no longer a heartbeat, and left the room.

My internal world shattered at that moment. I knew this pregnancy offered my last chance to have a baby, and I felt paralyzed with the magnitude of this emotional tsunami. In those initial moments and for a long time after, I couldn't begin to imagine how this gaping hole in my core could ever heal.

After walking through desperate situations like this one, I can look back and see the way opportunities developed in my life. I recognize how new doors opened when it looked like every single door was not only slammed shut but also securely bolted.

We face challenges in any season and at any age. Life also includes times of tweaking and seeking that require taking a deep, brave breath in order to jump into the pool of the unknown. Part of our seasoning develops when we are open to obtaining wisdom from the tough times and finding growth by stretching outside of our known environment.

What do we do when our dreams don't come to pass?

We dream of living next door to our long-term bestie and raising kids, but we can't have children. Our son or daughter dies before they reach adulthood. The grandkids who live close by move away. What happens when the life we envisioned takes an unimaginable turn?

We might look at the situation from a different angle or completely reshape how we proceed with our realities. Reframing doesn't just come in those mountainous majorly-impact-us-for-the-rest-of-our-life ways. Other people around us may not comprehend the depth of a seemingly simple loss.

Knowing we will face uncertainty and shaky portions of our journey, let's prepare beforehand (and during and after) to learn practical, healthy ways to work through these times and walk out defining steps of bravery and hope.

Desire for Gifts Beyond Our Reach

For at least two years of my childhood, my favorite Christmas song was "All I Want for Christmas Is My Two Front Teeth." I remember sitting on my grandfather's lap admiring the multi-colored lights and tinsel on our Christmas tree and singing the song while waiting for my big girl front teeth to finally grow in.

You see, at five or six years old, I jumped on the bed under the watchful eyes of my older siblings and several cousins. Our parents left them in charge of the youngest (me) with strict instructions to *not jump on the bed*!

Well, as soon as the door closed, they ignored me and I began to have fun jumping on the bed. Eventually, I fell off and knocked my two front baby teeth back up into my gums, which resulted in an emergency trip to a dentist and eventual oral surgery.

In addition, a *long* delay in tooth growth.

That's why for two years, all I wanted for Christmas was my two front teeth.

Around age ten, I found a game that I was certain I couldn't live without. It was called Mr. Marblehead or something like that—I can't even remember the name now. But, I do remember getting under the Christmas tree to find any present with my name on the tag that might be the size of that game.

One day I found a box just the right size. It had to be the Marblehead game. For the next couple of weeks, every chance I had, I grabbed that box and shook it to hear the lovely sound of marbles rolling around.

Christmas morning, I could barely stand it! I wanted to play that game. When I finally had the package in my hands and ripped the paper off, I sat and stared in amazement.

Not the good kind.

You see, what I unwrapped wasn't the Marblehead game at all. A popcorn popper sat on the floor instead of my greatly desired game. And even worse? A large broken piece lay inside the popper. It was all my fault. The daily shaking had taken its toll.

All I wanted for Christmas was the Marblehead game.

That feeling of want, disappointment, and despair played out in my adulthood many times as well.

Years later, I wanted a child. In the middle of several years of infertility, I remember praying and asking God to bless me with pregnancy and the healthy birth of a child.

All I wanted for Christmas was a baby of my own.

Another year, all I wanted for Christmas was for my father to be alive to celebrate with our family one more time.

Some years I wanted trivial things; in others, all I wanted was deliverance from barrenness or mourning or loneliness. Several involved wanting good health and healing for loved ones.

Many Christmas presents we want include material things while others are intangibles.

A job.
A car.
A place to live.
Toys.
Clothes.
Loved ones back in the fold of family.
Money to pay bills.
A family.

Sometimes, all we want for Christmas is for something painful and difficult to be removed.

Loneliness.
Depression.
Addiction.

Pain.

Grief.

Unforgiveness.

Bitterness.

The Christmas season is rooted in the anticipation and celebration of the babe born in a manger—the King of Kings and Lord of Lords. In our humanness, we can lose sight of the true meaning of Christmas.

During painful life seasons, sometimes we can barely put one foot in front of the other, much less focus on the reason for the season. This is especially true when we feel alone.

Blessed by God's Intangibles

Have you ever been in an impossible situation or even been in a "meh" mood because of what you feel is missing from your life? Then you see someone's post or picture with some version of "I am so blessed" or "#blessed?"

I've seen this play out not only on social media but also during in-person conversations. When something good happens in our life or when we just want to express gratitude, we often send a message or post a picture with the caption, "I am blessed" or "blessed."

In conversations, I hear over and over again similar reactions, especially from single friends. "I'm single and happy. I'd like to meet the right person, but I'm content. Yet every time I see a friend get engaged or married and use blessed in the caption, I feel less than and like I am missing out. Then I ask, 'Am I not blessed in my current reality?'"

I had another conversation with someone who said, "I don't have my parents here on Earth any longer. When I see pictures of people with their mothers or fathers and how they set aside days to honor them captioned with the words, 'I am so blessed,' I question whether or not I'm blessed."

Are we blessed by God with good things and people? Yes! We can experience his beauty and grace in our world each and every day.

In an effort to love others well, what if we considered the intangibles from God as blessings and the people, positions, and things that not everyone will have in this life as things for which we express our gratitude?

I've learned that the holiday season particularly highlights my lack when everyone else seems to have the people, things, or events that my heart desires but which I find absent in my own reality.

Whether you are on top of the world with joy or at the bottom of the heap buried in worry and grief, know this . . .

You are loved.

You are not alone.

Reach out to someone you know and love and tell them what they mean to you.

Step out by going to a Christmas service at a place of worship, watch online, or tune in to broadcast services on Christmas Eve.

All I *want* to want for Christmas this year (and every year in the future) is for us to grab onto the peace, love, and joy promised that long ago, holy night. "For today in the city of David there has been born for you a Savior, who is Christ the Lord" (Luke 2:11).

Life Preparation

No matter where we are in the midst of the fallout or preparation, we can't always stand ready for the surprises that knock us off our foundation. But often, by going through one storm, we learn ways to better set necessities in place for the next one.

For instance, we do need a practical, simple plan for natural disasters. Start by putting together an emergency "go" bag with essentials that you might need and keep it somewhere accessible.

Evaluate your location and common weather and disaster events that might take place in your region. Do you live in a flood area? What steps can you take to get together essentials, keep them in a user-friendly place where you live, and walk through a plan with everyone in your house? Not in a fearful, scary way, just a simple step-action plan that everyone can understand and know what they need to do.

Just as we need to prepare for these natural disasters, we also need to take steps to evaluate and prepare for other kinds of life events we might encounter.

Our basic understanding of how our history influenced us, our pursuit of who we desire to be, and shoring up good mental, physical, spiritual, emotional, and financial health will offer great benefits for our life storm prep.

The timeframe after an upsetting event feels unsettling and confusing. Reinforcing an overall healthy life mentality establishes a good practice before something happens. If you find yourself in the middle of the unsettled and haven't ever done this, begin right now!

Life Mentality

Have you ever known anyone with a "vitality of life" mentality? Their zest sparkles and infiltrates everything they do. Not a false or fake personality, just someone who lives life to the fullest, in big ways or small.

When we live with a "death" mentality, full of stress and worry, constant thoughts of what *will* or *might* go wrong in the future begin to impact everything. They might seem tiny at first, but they begin to direct our steps without our even realizing how they flavor choices, activities, and expectations of our present and future.

Dealing with the everyday impact of disease or physical limitations offers a reality for daily existence. But imagining or projecting something onto our future that is not rooted in our real-life setting influences our thoughts, responses, choices, and ability to dream unhindered.

The imagined negatives immediately place a false shadow on what isn't even there. So, let's affirm a life mentality and begin practicing the positive and good, allowing these thoughts to play in the background as optimistic ammunition to fight the dark negativity and keep it from creeping into our thoughts.

Let's take steps to fully live. This doesn't mean we need to do something grandiose each day. It means adopting an attitude that embraces the day God gives us. It means we must commit to being thankful and present in the moment with those we love.

Let's make every effort to stop autopilot or numb emotions!

Sometimes we might need to limit news and social media. Our online activity can become habitual and mindless. Consider setting a timer to get your attention and keep you from getting sucked into a fog of unintentional scrolling.

Let's shut the mental door on negativity or, better yet, take negative thoughts and add some hopeful optimism to them.

Another of my favorite Bible verses is "Finally, brethren, whatever is true, whatever is honorable, whatever is right, whatever is pure, whatever is lovely, whatever is of good repute, if there is any excellence and if anything worthy of praise, dwell on these things" (Philippians 4:8). It reminds me to dwell on thoughts that act as a foundation for a healthy life mentality.

A Closer Look: The Winds of Single Seasons

Sometimes singleness can seem like an overwhelming, ongoing, challenging winter blast.

In a podcast conversation with Lacey and Angela, we walked through healthy steps to take when we find ourselves in a state of singleness.[7] Many of our conclusions can be applied to any season of life.

We agreed that one good question to ask ourselves is, "What does God want me to do right here in this time of singleness?"

What do we do when our life isn't what we dreamed or expected? How do we live out our reality in this moment of time? So often, we can find ourselves trapped in periods of not waiting well—instead, looking to the future only and planning what we will do and become when we are finally *there*.

But what can we do to counter these feelings and overcome the drought we might feel to live our best lives in all seasons? Especially in the season of singleness?

Angela wisely reminded us that there are ebbs and flows with our feelings and situations. "There are times where it's going to be fine, and there are times where it's going to be hard. It's not that I have it figured out and I'm totally fine. You know, there are days that are hard, there are seasons that are hard, and so, I think not just rushing through those hard times and saying things like, 'Oh no, it's totally fine, everything's great.' Or shaming yourself—that you shouldn't feel sad or lonely."[8]

As we discussed this, I agreed and talked about not feeling like we must be on a timeline and avoid saying *should* to yourself. You *shouldn't* do this, or you s*houldn't* do that, or you *should* do this or that. Angela elaborated on this in a wonderful way.

> "You're not supposed to *should* all over yourself. We don't have to *should* anything. And so, when people say, 'You *should* be on whatever dating site," maybe it's time for you to, but maybe it's not. I will say there is not a formula. Things don't work the same way every time I get into the sad feelings. There are times to plan around Valentine's Day. There are times when I know I cannot go to the grocery store on February 12th, 13th, or 14th because it's an explosion of flowers, chocolate, and romantic dinner kits. So, I just have to plan that I'm going to go before or after. After, I can get cheap chocolate . . . it's great! Maybe avoid commercials or romantic comedies. Maybe stay off social media for a few days. Sometimes we might want to see them and celebrate, and sometimes it is hard. Give ourselves grace; both are okay."[9]

When we know ourselves and how to have healthy boundaries with outside interactions, we can celebrate and gather with friends. Celebrating and supporting one another helps stop the competition and comparison. Let's all be supportive. Find your safe people. The ones who offer space to cry, laugh, or simply sit quietly, and find creative ways to hang out together.

Lacey offers wise words for how to maintain a healthy understanding of ourselves.

> "We have to get out of comparative suffering. Comparison just brings judgment, punishment, and shame

storms. We have to stop comparing our suffering. Defensiveness and anger: We must look at the root and take responsibility. Discontentment can come from not feeling seen, valuable, or secure. God speaks security, value, and being seen. Once we know that, we can have honest conversations with others. I'm responsible for my own feelings, but I want to let you into my life, I want to be vulnerable, I want to give that person a chance to see me and hopefully respond in love but, I can tell them when you say, 'xyz,' I feel 'xyz.' Hopefully, that stops hard questions, often not. Look for the root of discomfort within ourselves. Again, know ourselves. Be inviting, not finger-pointing. Be gracious and not reactive when someone posts a benign or offensive question or comment. When it hurts our feelings, we don't need to react. We can offer to let them see how they hurt us. Vulnerability and honesty equal intimacy in our friendships and relationships. Our primary need is with the Lord, but we also mature as people when we can do this with them. I don't know if this is forever or just for today. What if my healthiness is rooted in my singleness?"[10]

During our conversation, both Lacey and Angela touched on the need to take it a day at a time. Don't *should* yourself, and don't compare. Make a plan for questions or comments, be kind and inviting. Welcome people who you trust into the intimate spaces. God transforms our lives; we thrive and we seek to live purposeful lives right where we are instead of thinking ahead to next month or year. We are called to live where he has us right now to the best of our ability while looking to him and leaning on him. It is up to us to seek and find ways to have a relationship with God and to seek people who have strong faith and are grounded in their singleness. We all want to live our best life every day—our specific, wonderful purpose.

Don't wait. Live your life.

Chapter Four

How Do We See Ourselves?

*A*s a young child, I learned I was an "unexpected." A family friend shared this information with me.

As an adult, I have a better understanding of our family situation at the time. My parents had two children and purchased their "dream" ranch-style home. The 1,800-square-foot house had three bedrooms and two baths. A perfect size for their small family.

Right after they moved in, they found out they were pregnant with me.

My brother is seven years older. Not too far into my young childhood, he began telling me that my parents found me in a trashcan. Behind their backs, he would say, "Look around, you don't look like anyone in this family!"

I began to stare at my sister, wondering if I could see ways we looked alike. My sister, ten years older, seemed so glamorous and grown up.

Since the two of us shared a room, I often watched her sitting in front of her big lighted makeup mirror. She spent a lot of time studying her image, rolling her hair with hot rollers or orange juice cans (popular at the time) or applying her false eyelashes and grabbing her "fall" (detachable hairpiece) off its Styrofoam head and putting it on before a date.

As I spent many hours observing her behavior and studying her features, I realized I certainly didn't look like her. Our differences created confusion in my young brain. When she was spending her teenage time experimenting with her looks, I was still a kid. I lived an outdoor, active life—climbing trees, riding my bike, playing in the yard with friends, riding horses, and running through pastures at our farm.

On a normal day, you would find me with messy, tangled hair or with lopsided pigtails. Most of the time, I wore a just-stained T-shirt and had scraped or scabbed knees.

I laugh at myself now when I think about the mental confusion in my six-year-old brain. Of course, one would notice very little resemblance between sixteen-year-old and six-year-old girls.

The irony of my brother's relentless teasing about my identity? As a child and also as an adult, I look just like the boys in my family. There's no denying the resemblance between my dad, my brother, and myself.

When I was a child, Sunday school teachers taught me to sing, "Jesus loves me, this I know." They helped lay a strong foundation of God's love in my life. (A big shout-out to those who take time to spend Sunday mornings with the littles in church. You plant seeds for life!)

What is the God-truth about who we are? We must know this to know how to live. I am still learning to recognize who I am in Christ and to know the truth of his image in me. I might not have been planned by my family, but I was most definitely planned by my God.

You were too.

Intergenerational Impact

After I finished guest teaching a Sunday school class, I stood at the front talking with several people. The lesson included Scripture study and application about who we are in Christ and together in our church community. As an illustration, I shared the story of my "unexpected" arrival in my family.

While standing and talking, an elderly man and woman approached, tears streaming down his face. He introduced his wife, himself, and then told me he was eighty-five years old. He wanted to let me know how much it meant to him to hear my story, and it touched him deeply because of his own "unexpected" start in life.

He proceeded to tell me about his parents and their struggle with the Great Depression. He shared about how his father demanded that his mother have an abortion when she discovered she was pregnant with him (the gentleman standing before me). It felt gut-wrenching to hear this man describe the love his mother had for him and how she stood up to his father and refused. There were more details shared and lots of emotion expressed in this short conversation with a stranger.

He seemed to feel comforted by telling me his story and emphasized the importance of the lesson we'd just discussed regarding family, friends, and community. Over and over, he told me how grateful he felt to know that someone else had an unexpected arrival into a family, and his wife looked relieved to see him share the story.

I've thought about this situation many times since then. When we share our stories and experiences, we learn that others have walked interesting, sometimes painful, often confusing, paths too.

What healthy bonding we experience when we share, listen, and offer empathy to one another!

Understanding Yourself

However your life began, wherever your past led, no matter the labels, ideas, and comparisons that formed around and in you long ago, you are a treasured child of God.

As we rise and start each day and see our image in the mirror, let's remember: We need to know who we are to know how to live—we are each a unique, beloved creation made in the image of Almighty God.

If you stand in a different place with your faith, will you allow me to encourage you to remember your great worth?

We can explore our history of people and messages, looking back with curiosity to gain a better understanding of ourselves. Not to get stuck or to blame, just to have more clarity about past events, people, and their influence.

> I love my family, and we have shared lots of joy and pain as well as ups and downs through the years. I'm really grateful to call my brother and sister close friends in life, and we have each other's backs! And I know my parents truly loved me and considered me one of the greatest delights of their lives!

We must know who we are to fully *live*, to discover all the possibilities that are ours, and to fulfill the purpose of our creation. So often in life, we don't take the time to know ourselves. We rely on what others tell us about how we were raised, what we were taught, and about the expectations that were placed on us by others in order to fulfill what they wanted.

Let's invest some time and ask ourselves:

- What do I want?
- Who am I?
- What are my passions?
- What are my skills?
- What things did I do in childhood that I enjoyed?

I am passionate about encouraging you to explore these areas because I've watched many people who don't know, ask, explore, or investigate. In fact, I've often neglected to do these things in my own life.

We can pour ourselves into taking care of other people or fulfilling our work or community responsibilities, but how often do we take a time-out with ourselves? We get to know other people in our lives, especially those we love and with whom we do life.

Do we invest that same curiosity or knowledge in ourselves? This isn't a selfish or self-absorbed mindset but rather a valiant effort to know ourselves and make the most of this life and the time we've been given.

You are a unique individual created for this time and place. You're treasured, gifted, beautiful, and beloved. Give yourself the gift of effort and time to gain a better understanding of yourself.

Yes, this can be a little unnerving, but it is well worth it. We can make bold discoveries about what makes us tick, what sparks our imagination, what emboldens our courage, and in what ways we spend the valuable time we have here on Earth making a positive difference.

Often it takes reflecting on a past storm or having the residual effects pop up out of nowhere to help us explore, gain a better understanding, and find freedom.

Freedom in Letting Go

I spent years on an infertility journey, and for much of that time, I felt numb. Lots of time went by when I didn't even recognize my need to invest in my emotional recovery and intentional life choices.

Some of the underlying pain kept me emotionally and mentally enslaved without my realizing it.

My infertility journey involved several years, numerous doctors, untold tests, lots of needles, and humiliation. I was faced with overwhelming information while focusing my attention on every aspect of life and the goal of getting pregnant, carrying to term, and giving birth to a healthy baby.

It. Was. A. Long. Road.

A third pregnancy offered the longest timeframe of hope. Then that too was lost. Due to my age and several physical situations, I knew it was time to lay the dream down and leave it behind.

It sounds easier when I sum it up for you! This was a long process.

I eventually surrendered my dream of being a mom, sobbed and mourned, and in time took baby steps on the new path that was opened up by God. (Ironic, right? Baby steps were required in order to move forward after my inability to have a child.)

One day, after walking through several years of learning to live with the outcome in healthy ways, I spoke with a younger relative, who is also a close friend. She commented on how she'd seen a new side of healing in me. I thought about her encouragement and decided to fully embrace the future and keep moving forward with purpose.

Several days after that conversation, I opened a cabinet in the bathroom and a half-used bottle of lotion fell out. As I looked over the wooden shelves, I noticed the long-neglected infertility corner on the bottom—miscellaneous treatment items quietly taking up space.

For ten years, I'd reached for items beside and above the boxes of medicine, the unopened syringes, and other leftover infertility paraphernalia that cluttered my cabinet and my life. I had become so used to seeing them that I didn't notice them anymore.

Because of the conversation with my relative, I immediately began a total purging of that cabinet. As I went through the shelves and threw away old lotions and sunblock, recycled old boxes of hair gadgets and products, I kept glancing down at the corner containing my painful past.

Then I stopped, realizing that as long as I avoided the expired infertility corner, I would never be free of it.

The time had come.

As I threw each package into the pharmacy biohazard bag, my internal load lightened bit by bit. When I let go of the last item, I felt momentarily and completely unburdened. The invisible infertility chains clattered to the floor.

Never would I have guessed the level of freedom I'd find by disposing of the medical reminders of the years of pain, disappointment, and loss.

I will never "get over" not being a mom, but I can take charge of how the loss affects me and not allow the loss to enslave me emotionally, physically, and spiritually. God doesn't want me paralyzed in pain. I was created with a purpose, and my life has meaning. The longing for my motherhood dream will never disappear completely, but it can be redirected.

Once the corner of my cabinet was laid bare, the fresh breeze of internal freedom filled me, and from that day forward, the heaviness of overlooked items lightened and drifted away.

Often, it isn't just those visual obstacles that remind us of the personal junk we might need to work on purging. Sometimes literal storms trigger reactions that painfully remind us we have heart issues that might need a little work.

When we mine our history, sometimes we have to do some "heart" work.

Chapter Five

Heartitude

*O*ne afternoon, I found myself in the middle of a different kind of storm.

Literally.

Physically, mentally, emotionally, spiritually.

I sat behind the steering wheel of my car on a local freeway, trying desperately to get to a medical facility before they closed. One of my dogs had undergone emergency exploratory surgery, and I needed to speak with the vet about the procedure he'd performed that day. The entire week had centered around a health crisis and for several days involved trips to emergency veterinary hospitals at all hours and dire, seemingly unstoppable weight loss in a small pup who only weighed seventeen pounds to begin with.

My sweet dog had to be picked up by a certain time that afternoon, and I needed information on how to best care for him that night. I desperately sought answers to the chronic issue.

For some reason, the post-surgery call from the vet hospital went straight to my voicemail. When I called back, there was no answer. So, I decided to get in the car and head to the hospital as the drive was only about twenty minutes in good weather and light traffic.

Suddenly, at the same time I entered the freeway, the weather shifted, and a massive storm moved overhead. I found myself clenching the steering wheel tightly as the heavens opened up and pouring rain created areas of standing water on the road.

Traffic was horrible, and my twenty-minute drive quickly transformed into something much longer.

On top of the unstable conditions, there came an additional communication challenge. I kept hitting redial (hands-free!) on the phone, but no one answered in the medical facility. It just rang and rang.

Within a few minutes, I became extremely stressed over the storm, driving conditions, timing, medical news, inability to communicate with the doctor or staff, and the build-up of other vehicles in my way.

While trying to make my way through stop-and-go traffic and pouring down rain, I kept hitting redial . . . over and over and over. Still no answer.

Time kept moving forward while I wasn't. Sheets of rain were now forming dangerous flood spots on the freeway, but I didn't care.

When an occasional space opened up, I squeezed in, gripping the steering wheel, rushing through standing water, and persistently touching redial for the call.

All the while, I was trying to get my over-the-top-panic under control.

I realized my stress level was rising, so I began to pray out loud, begging God.

Pleas of please became my cry . . .

Please let me get there in time.
Please get me there, safely.
Please help them answer the phone.
Please get these other cars out of my way.

Have you ever been there?
Then, suddenly, my pleas and begging became demands . . .

Lord, you are all-powerful, make these cars get out of my
way; I MUST get there soon.
Lord, make them answer the phone.
Lord, stop this storm.
Lord, move my car as fast as possible.

My tone and attitude really began to escalate as I became more
fearful and anxious.
Then . . .
Everything began to verbally erupt in angry accusations *at* God.

Lord, why didn't you stop "this" two years ago?
Jesus, why didn't you fix "that" five years ago?
God, where were you in the situation with no solution ten
years ago?

I quickly realized my pleas of please became angry discontent in a matter of minutes and recognized that I had never
fully dealt with several unsettling life circumstances. I'd shoved
them down so far that they simmered over time and turned to

grievances against God because he didn't change or fix them to my liking.

I started listing them at the top of my lungs—I had no idea they were still taking up real estate inside of me. These grievances turned anger had become little weeds rooted in my heart . . . and I felt so ashamed.

Once I listened to what was blowing out of me, I stopped and immediately began apologizing to the Lord.

I was devastated by my behavior and by the realization that all of *that* had lived in me for so long. I thought I had dealt with everything long before.

While I cried and asked his forgiveness, I began to pray for him to uproot those weeds of anger, discontent, and bitterness from deep within. As if the water on my windshield wasn't enough to hinder my vision, I cried so hard I could hardly see through my own river of tears.

God and I had some gardening work to do. This was soul-deep work that I couldn't do in my own power. I needed Holy Spirit power and cleansing to work through and finally deal with these issues in a healthy, God-involved way.

Have you ever had soul-deep anger about something or about a situation that didn't work out the way you planned?

A job loss?
Wayward child?
Marital struggles?
Health issue?
Addiction?
Singleness?
Widowhood?

Abandonment?

Financial Situation?

Conflict with someone?

One of the ways I've found to work through difficult self-examination lies in studying biblical wisdom to grow closer to the Lord, become more Christlike, and live out his purposes in my life.

What we do with our anger determines what our anger does to us.

The further I travel in life, the more importance I place on what I've learned (and it's an ongoing process!). By choosing to be shaped by God's truth, my understanding grows, and so does the wisdom that gives me true freedom to live a flourishing life.

I finally made it to the hospital that day. It took an hour and a half, and thankfully the surgeon was still there. It turned out their incoming phone lines were not working due to the storm. I gathered the information I needed about my pup's chronic disease, got medications and a treatment plan, and headed home.

I sat in the car, grasping the steering wheel. Started the car and drove in silence. The outside storm had passed and the freeway was deserted. As my four-legged child curled up and rested in the backseat, I used that time to have an earnest, internal conversation with God about the deep-rooted anger I had discovered in my heart that day.

A new day came, and I phoned a trusted friend who has known me forever. She knew about all the challenges I'd faced and evidently still had residual bitterness about. In our conversation, I was repentant and sorrowful that they still had a hold on me at all.

She said, "Don't feel like you haven't made progress. Sometimes it just takes more time to deal with deeper layers of issues."

If you find yourself needing some heart work, consider taking ten minutes of quiet time this week (schedule it on the calendar if you need to) and pray about areas in which you know you're holding onto anger or bitterness (maybe relentless fear?). Also, pray about areas that still need a bit of recognition.

Investigate where your heart garden needs to be cleared of weeds. Take those first steps to process and purge. It might help to include a trusted friend for accountability. Maybe set up a coffee meet to share ways to work through issues.

What we do with our anger determines what our anger does to us.

Let's take the necessary steps to find and deal with these areas so we can move forward with lighter steps and freer hearts.

So, what can we do about our anger? We can perceive, process, and purge.

Perceive

We must recognize that we are holding onto anger. This requires taking time and paying attention to our responses during stressful situations.

We have busy days with constant input, and that can create edgy layers that contribute to developing anger.

Take a decluttering step with activities, commitments, and interpersonal and personal issues to help alleviate underlying ripples. Dedicate a piece of your schedule to consider how much time and attention you allow yourself to devote to anything outside your basics of home, family, and work.

You can also take a healthy step by reserving some quiet time to think, consider, pray, and ask, "What makes me angry? What is my intended goal in my anger?"

There once was a little boy who had a bad temper. His father wanted to help the boy understand the ramifications of his words, anger, and relationships. He instructed the boy to hammer a nail in the fence every time he lost his temper. Many days later, after much hammering, the boy decided to control his temper instead of hammering.

One day he came home to report to his dad that he didn't lose his temper. His father then said he could remove a nail each day he controlled his temper. After many days, he finally removed all the nails and went to celebrate with his dad.

They went back out to the fence and the father pointed out the scars and holes left by the nails in the wooden fence. He explained to his son that he was proud of his growth in that area and wanted to show him the damage that angry words can leave behind. He could remove the nails but not the holes.[11]

What do our wooden fences look like?

Have our words left holes in our fences?

We live in an unfriendly world. Divisiveness rules the day, and people seem to stay poised with their devices, ready to respond, comment, or write a retort to anything they see on social media.

Civil conversation seems to be a thing of the past.

Believers in Jesus Christ are called to offer good words for edification, to give grace, to not grieve the Holy Spirit, and to be kind and forgive each other as God, in Christ, forgives us.

What is our goal when we let anger build? Do we seek to cancel and destroy those with whom we disagree? Jesus calls us to validate others in love, not only in the body of Christ, but also in how we show him to the world.

Once we take time to perceive our anger and what it looks like for us, we determine how to process our anger.

Process

How we process anger is crucial to determine ahead of time—before someone hits our hot button or before we have a knee-jerk reaction. I'm not saying this is easy, but I've found it is necessary to work through internal anger ahead of time.

One day I was riding on a steam engine train. The train's power came from burning coal and water and as the train journeyed along, ash and embers occasionally flew into the air.

Behind it, I noticed a much smaller vehicle speeding along the railroad tracks. I affectionately call this a tut-tut (I don't know the official name). Two people riding in this little car have a water tank on board. They ride behind the train and look for places where burning embers fall and start little fires. They are on the lookout to do damage control, to stop and put the small fires out before they take off and damage the surrounding national forest.

When we leave sparks in the path behind us, we can also leave a trail of regret.

During the journey, the train stopped and began to blow off steam. I heard a man describing the action to someone behind me, explaining, "The train is blowing off steam to let some of the heat out so the pressure doesn't cause an explosion in the engine."

This train offers a great analogy for relieving the pressure of our anger.

Do we move through life throwing off ash and burning embers that require others to come along behind us and put out the small fires? Or do we process through our words, deeds, and potential anger by finding healthy ways to "blow off steam" and work through internal anger with God and with trusted friends in community?

If we aren't productive and proactive in our dealings with anger, we can do irreparable damage to others and ourselves.

What we do with our anger determines what our anger does to us.

After we perceive and determine our process for anger, then we go about the work to purge.

Purge

I grew up believing that anger wasn't acceptable (I'm not sure where this came from), and directly or indirectly, learned to shove angry emotions as far down as possible.

To keep the lid on them.

But when we do that, we forget. Anger, like fire, can burn. It can simmer quietly for a long time.

But, as often happens with something left cooking too long or too hot, our quietly simmering pot of anger can bubble and boil over. It can ruin the inside of the pot and surrounding stovetop.

We lead healthier lives when we recognize and acknowledge our anger (justified or not) and pray for God's strength and guidance as we work through it.

All of this perceiving and processing and purging of anger must be bookended in prayer, before, during, and after. We also need to seek accountability with those close in our community. We must spend time in prayer, reflection, and honest self-assessment, inviting others we trust into the midst of this activity.

Often there may be a righteous issue where we feel called by God to support and do something. We can purge the unhelpful anger but let it also drive us to positive, loving action.

What is our anger about?

Is it something that we just need to pray about and let go, or is it brought on by a serious wrong done by someone? If so, pray for the Holy Spirit's work in us to come to a place of forgiveness for them and what they did.

Please hear me.

Forgiveness encompasses a huge topic with lots of layers. If someone caused harm, what they did was not okay. What we are working through here is how to deal with *our* anger. In other words, by dealing with our heart issues, we control how much damage we allow our anger to do to us and to others.

If we spend a long time allowing a hurt, personal injustice, or life disappointment to fester, one day we might find ourselves in a panic on a freeway dealing with an unexpected internal storm. The same is true if we invest time and energy into continually avoiding it instead of working through the pain. We might be in need of weeding the gardens of our hearts and spirits.

At the top of my go-to list of Bible verses is, "Trust in the Lord with all your heart and do not lean on your own understanding. In all your ways acknowledge him, and he will make your paths straight" (Proverbs 3:5–6).

I'm adding in verse 7: "Do not be wise in your own eyes; fear the Lord and turn away from evil."

Often our anger is a result of fear and distrust. When life doesn't turn out as expected, we can fear what will happen. That fear overwhelms us as we realize we aren't in control of the outcome, leading us to become angry and frustrated with the loss of control.

Our anger can also result in great distrust. The unexpected happens and we grow angry at the outcome. Why did our Lord not act to stop this from happening?

Look at Proverbs 3:5–7 again.

Trust with *all* your heart.
Don't lean on your *own* understanding.
In *all* our ways acknowledge him.
Don't be wise in our *own* eyes.

Trust him.
Lean on him.
In all ways acknowledge him.
Find our wisdom in him.

For God so loved the world, he gave his only son. For you.
For me.
Do we perceive, process, and purge our anger and turn in
trust to him?

He sees our fear.
He understands our mistrust.
He empathizes with our impatience.
He weeps with us in our pain.
He is the balm for our anger.

Learning what to do with our anger through perceiving, processing, and purging is not a one-time or one-day event. As we
journey through life, we encounter ongoing opportunities to address
these little weeds in our hearts.

Creating Breaks

So often, demanding schedules prevent us from taking time to think
through challenging anger areas. In the western culture of America,
spring break comes around each year, usually in March. For most,

it signals vacation time while celebrating the entrance to spring and warmer weather.

No matter the age or season in life, we all need a spring break. Spring offers a time of renewal as we exit the dormancy of a long wintry season indoors.

The world around us hums (on a good day) with busyness and clangs (on a chaotic day) with relentless chatter. In the midst of "helpful" technology and thriving work, sometimes we forget to push the pause button, much less the off button.

We were not created for the constancy of doing. We are human beings, and in order to experience quality life, we must embrace timely breaks before we effectively break down.

What could this look like in our lives?

At the end of the day, shut down technology for one hour. If you have a family, go outside and play with your kids. If you are single, go for a walk or meet up face to face with friends over a cup of coffee.

Pick up a book. Yes, one of those printed, bound objects with lots of words on the page. Hold it in your hands and be transported to another world for a brief time.

Sit outside, close your eyes, and listen to the world around you. What do you hear? The breeze blowing? Bees buzzing? Birds singing? Leaves rustling in the trees? Cars rushing by? A distant horn?

Be still and know. Clear your mind. If you are a person of faith, be still and know that God IS.

Spend time in the Bible with this verse, "For we are his workmanship, created in Christ Jesus for good works, which God prepared beforehand so that we would walk in them" (Ephesians 2:10).

Go outside. Explore the natural world. Get your feet wet. Look at plants and flowers. Stop and feel the bark of a tree.

We were created for a purpose, and we were also designed to rest. Constant stress, worry, and activity offer the illusion of importance and meaning, but these deceptions can often cause deep internal damage and unrest within our souls.

The next time you feel the tensions of life rising, get outside and take a walk. Think of the little things in life that please your heart and senses. Ponder all of the areas in life where thankfulness blooms.

Taking a break can keep us from breaking.

Learning to break gives us the time and space to work through difficult thoughts and experiences. Taking a pause might also lead to a renewed passion for overcoming obstacles, inspiring us to pursue the plans we thought had disappeared.

Chapter Six

Back to Foundation Basics

The sun beat down on the small group as they created the foundation outline of the house.

I stood ready to help but knew nothing about construction and could see that the crew had their actions down to a science. The rudimentary plumb line practice, used to measure and square the walls, captivated me.

The builders had no power tools or modern instruments. They weren't setting up the level foundation for a large dwelling but for a small cinderblock house (maybe 10x15 feet). It would house a family currently living in a hazardous environment with nothing for protection except salvaged pieces of metal, soft materials, tree branches, and pieces of rope.

As I watched, they took turns holding a long, clear, flexible plastic tube partially filled with water. As the tube stretched along the straight line of the set foundation or from each corner diagonally to the next, they carefully checked that the water reflected the level balance. They meticulously made adjustments until they had a set plumb line. It took time, attention, care, and precision.

Their focus on this process showed their care for one another. Time spent poring over the plumb line for this tiny dwelling underlined the importance of having a good foundation on which to build. It didn't matter to them that their construction site was small. They didn't give up because of discomfort or time. Each person involved in this stage gave every effort to ensure the stability of the foundation they wanted to build.

This building project would eventually give the intended family private living space and safety from weather and from ever-present rats. These beginning steps eventually transformed a literal dump into a neighborhood of families in a third-world area.

I watched careful, precise movements and slight adjustments, over and over, feeling moved by their willingness to establish a solid space for their friends and neighbors.

Not only can we take care helping to build home foundations for our friends, neighbors, community, and ourselves, but we can also invest time building solid life foundations for work, action, character, and habits.

Corner Posts of Life

I sat motionless at my father's memorial service, listening to one of his lifelong friends describe him as a corner post in the fence line of life. Tears gathered in my eyes and rolled down my cheeks as I heard the essence of my dad summed up in this gracious and accurate metaphor. I heard words like stability, strength, foundation, anchor, balance, and support.

If you've spent any time in the country or around farmland, you will immediately understand. I'm a half-city, half-farm girl, and I watched my dad build barbed wire fences over many weekends through the years.

I didn't do well in physics class and had no clue about things like engineering. Before his funeral service, I really had no understanding of the value of a corner post along the fence line. Hearing this gave me a new appreciation for all of the post holes I watched him manually dig and the fences I saw him build. The comparison of those actions and their results to how he lived his overall life made me proud and deeply moved.

All of us are flawed human beings, and we will never live a life of perfection, but we can strive for excellence, flourishing, and leaving a mark of stability, support, love, and grace in this world. As we search the areas of our lives for opportunities to grow and develop, we can prioritize making a positive influence on our corners of the world. We can renew the desire and effort to stand as corner posts in the social fence line of life.

How do we do this?

We can only change ourselves.

When we have a strong foundation, we enhance how we approach extraordinary events in our lives—the good, the bad, and the uncomfortable.

One of my pastor friends used to say, "If you aren't in the middle of a storm, there's one coming." He also advised staying ready and looking for God's blessings after the storm.

I've been through small dustups as well as a few life-changing, long-term events. I've learned that God will see us through storms and uncomfortable times. When he does, we experience his grace, glory, growth, and the opportunities we might never have encountered without the difficulties.

Chapter Seven

Plumb Line Steps

*O*ne of the key ways to gain solid footing for mild or fierce winds is to learn about ourselves. We must devote time to know who we are—starting right where we are—to gain a better understanding of how we will live joyful, steady lives to the best of our ability.

We mine our history and know where we came from, we take a look at our foundation and how we want to build on that, and then we get into the details. To get to the heart of your core self, walk through, think about, and answer the following questions about your life.

Looking Back to Move Forward

Let's take a look at some of the past events in your story, looking back on your life and working through a defining timeline. Begin by answering the questions below; then, we'll look at specific multi-year increments with detailed questions for those timeframes:

- Who helped you?
- What life influencing events happened—big or small?
- What challenged you?
- Who made you feel special? What did they do or say?
- When you were a child, which adults spoke into your life positively? Negatively?
- What did you like to do?
- What classes did you like?
- Did you have special teachers? Who were they?
- What activities did you do with your friends?
- What was your faith like?
- Camp, interests, clothes, activities, inspiration?
- What are your earliest memories of life challenges? What did you witness—how did adults behave?

Age 10–20 years old
Same questions plus:

- Where did you grow the most?
- Who encouraged you?
- Who helped you and affirmed you?
- How did you rebel?
- What extra activities did you have after school?

Age 20–30 years old
Same questions, plus:

- Where did you experience adulting?
- What decisions helped this?
- When did you first experience a life storm?

- What tapes played in your head that were put there from external circumstances? (Words of doubt, negativity, positivity, and joy.)

Life events, interests, passions, and other people all impact how we grow and develop, what we think, and how we define ourselves. When we look back at the influential people and events in life, we can gain a broader perspective on the real issues and lose the unhelpful or unnecessary.

We can't control what others do or say, but we can choose what we want to leave behind as we grow. When we become independent adults, we can choose either to fill ourselves with what others have said or to replace their words altogether. Often, we need to give ourselves permission to release unhelpful mental tapes, words, philosophies, and expectations.

If necessary, find a professional counselor or therapist to help you gain the tools to decide what enhances your coping skills and which negatives to release. Surround yourself with people you trust, those who will speak the truth in love.

Mining our day for thankfulness establishes a consistent step in our journey.

Thankfulness is the Key

When you read the word *campaign*, what is your first internal response? For many, it brings a sense of negativity and sometimes triggers frustration and stress.

Wonderful campaigns do exist: health awareness campaigns, pledge drives for worthy causes, campaigns to raise funds for schools, churches, and community organizations. All of these can earn our time, attention, and financial commitment.

But recent presidential campaign seasons have reminded me of the way unpleasantness can unfold on social media.

Many years ago, on an August day, I posted the following on one of my social media feeds: "Today, I contemplated quitting social media until after the elections. The growing number of divisive posts is quite disheartening. Instead, I resolve to counter the negativity by expressing thankfulness for something every day until November. Join me?"

To be honest, I felt more than disheartened. The rudeness and disrespect from all sides of numerous aisles felt shocking and overwhelming. People from every walk of life (including those in all forms of leadership positions) were hurling derogatory remarks at others in comment sections.

At the time, I wondered how we'd become a society and culture of such divisiveness and disrespect. Hiding behind a computer or phone screen does not give anyone license to wound with their words.

I almost ran in the other direction and gave up. Then the eternal optimist in me protested. I thought and prayed about what I could do and then determined to counter the contentious campaign with a kinder, gentler campaign that might add a little positivity to the social media circus.

I created a thankful post every day and asked others to share their thankful thought in the comments or just think about it on their own. Several people engaged with the posts each day and many called or emailed me to say thank you for sharing something positive. This campaign continued through the presidential election, and then I was finished.

Or so I thought.

A friend called and asked why I stopped. At the time, she'd been facing a massive health storm of a loved one as well as long-term grief for an overwhelming loss. She told me those posts were the only positive thing about her days and that I needed to continue. When I asked for how long, she replied, "Just keep posting."

So, I kept posting daily—for seven years.

I can't believe it went on that long. It was an incredible journey. A college friend I haven't seen since we were together in school wrote her thankful comment under my post every single day for those seven years. I had other friends in the community and church who would post with me several times a week and some who posted once a month.

Many never posted but instead sent emails, texts, or private messages. Several people stopped me out in public to tell me they read my posts every day and expressed how much they appreciated the reminder to be thankful.

There were many days when I felt like it was a useless task, that no one cared that I made the effort every day. Usually, those were the days I felt compelled to post anyway and would privately hear about how much my posts meant. I realized several things during these years:

> People watch what we put out there even when we don't think anyone pays attention. (So be careful what we post.)

> Thankfulness became a habit and ingrained in my day. Whether a large event or experience, or something simple in the day, I learned to find gratefulness in any situation. Knowing that I had a friend who was waiting for me to post every day so she could join me gave me daily purpose in the midst of personally challenging times.

Looking back at my thankful day posts, I can see patterns in my life, remember incredible experiences, and have an understanding of the bigger life picture during certain seasons.

Remembering what God has done, and what I've come through, reminds me to incorporate thankfulness into every day. It keeps me humble, dependent on God, and in a place of expectation to see what he has next.

I never scheduled my thankful posts ahead of time because I wanted to be in the moment every day. If I had a bad day, I had to really examine the day to find thankfulness.

On hard days when we struggle to give thanks, you and I can draw on at least one thankful thought—we are alive. Just as we need others to offer us encouragement and positivity, we need to give this to ourselves as well. We all need hope.

Sometimes it can feel scarce.

Other times gratitude comes easily.

When we make ourselves find something positive on a difficult day, it can help our spirit and change our mindset.

Since I stopped posting every day, I miss it. There was something transformative about intentionally thinking through the day, typing the words to generate the graphic, and uploading it onto my website to share on social media.

The process made me really think, what am I thankful for? Then I had to create something to represent my conclusion. Once I shared it, I knew there was at least one other person waiting for me to post because she wanted to share hers. Here we were, two friends separated by years, living in different cities with different lives, walking this virtual road together, encouraging each other.

When we can train our brain to look for and take the time to find something to be thankful for—to find the good each day—our default perspective launches healthy thoughts and attitudes. These thoughts and attitudes grow deep inner roots of good, wholesome, calm, strong, courageous responses for the next storm we will encounter.

We know something could be coming down the road. We don't live in fear or anticipation, we don't grow a hard shell of isolation or cynicism, we don't anticipate it, but we can prepare our minds and spirits for those days.

A thankful heart and a positive mind provide personal peace and a respectful, dignified public sharing of ideas and information. Let's bolster up and face the winds. If we wait until we're in the middle of difficulty and raw pain in our lives, we get caught up in overwhelming winds instead of having a foundation to help keep us steady.

Thankfulness is a necessity in my prayer life, especially when I find myself thinking too much about challenges of the world—culture, loneliness, pandemic, isolation. Counter the overwhelming negatives with your own thankfulness. Write in a journal, share a short daily text, or phone a friend who will commit to do this with you. Whatever works best for you.

Born of frustration, my "Thankfulday" habit developed into a daily evaluation of my heart. I started the campaign to influence a bit of social media for good. What really transpired was a change of heart within me.

I am so grateful for this lengthy lesson in thankfulness. It changed how I view events and people in my life, provided a beautiful connection with a long-ago friend, and gave daily reasons to rearrange my thoughts in a more positive manner.

As you have most likely experienced, the cultural and societal divide is wider than ever, and harsh words flying back and forth on social media seem to be the norm. In our general, everyday social media life, we have a great need for kind exchanges.

Will you join me in transforming a bit of social media into a positive and respectful place for discussion? We can make a difference and use our campaign for good.

The thankfulness campaign that became a daily habit for so long raised its positive head again when I so desperately needed to reframe and refocus.

Thankfulness After the Storm

After the horrific tornado, we were all working to clean up and organize needed repairs, and I vacillated between feeling defeated, exhausted, and in awe of the ways people came together to help one another.

I realized I needed to make a thankful list. So, I put on a thankful sweatshirt I bought during my campaign and wrote:

Thankful. Period.

Thankful for no deaths and few injuries in the storm.

Thankful for family you can call at 11:00 p.m. and say, "I have to evacuate." Their response, "C'mon." Thankful for strangers who provided rides out of the danger zone when there was no way in.

Thankful for the kind empathy from everyone working to clean up the overwhelming mess and destruction.

Thankful for electrical and gas employees who work overtime to restore comfort and order. Also, for those teams who left their families, homes, and communities to help ours.

Thankful for churches and other faith communities that jump into action to feed and care for, to love their neighbors—all of their neighbors.

Thankful for grocery stores, restaurants, and other businesses that ride in to feed and supply people in need.

Thankful for schools that send their students out in the community to help with whatever is needed.

Thankful for every human being who reflects the love and light of Jesus in the midst of stormy times and the lengthy aftermath.

My thankful list went on and on.

Kindness, unity, and care are more widespread in the reality of everyday life than we sometimes realize. May our steps each day remind us to look for the good and to be the good in the world around us.

During those bad recovery days, I clung to the hope of what would be someday. The recovering, remodeling, and rebuilding process still proceeds forward over two years later. I love the beautiful practice my friend Lacey shared about how she handles bad days.

The Bad Day Practice

Looking back to see how we made it through previous challenging circumstances can encourage us in present times of trouble. Lacey offered incredible advice[12] on dealing with difficult, bad days:

> I reflect on bad days in the past, and I think about how I got through those days and how painful it was in the moment, but now that I'm so far away, I can look back and see the goodness and grace and see that maybe I just survived. Maybe it doesn't make sense at all. Maybe it was the worst day of my life and it makes no sense, but I'm still here, I'm still alive, I'm okay. So, I think, on bad days now, I reflect on those bad days and reassure myself that I made it then, and I can make it now. If this becomes the new worst day of my life, then on the next bad day, I'll be able to reflect on that and know I'm okay. As humans, we are storytellers, and we talk to ourselves more than we talk to anyone else. Maybe it's not out loud, but we are constantly talking in our heads. We are wired and built to be storytellers. I find what helps me is to figure out what story I'm telling myself—what's the narrative I've created in my brain, and is that narrative actually based in reality? Then I can glean off other stories.

She then expressed how she looks at other women's lives to see what the Lord is doing in them and what their lives look like. This conversation reminded me again that younger women are watching even when we don't know it. Lacey elaborated, "What's helpful for me is listening to stories of how people overcame hardships. When you hear those stories, it starts to rewire your brain of what goodness and grace can be found; real change can happen, I'm not stuck in my misery forever."[13]

Hearing Lacey describe how she looks back on her own past experiences for current encouragement and why she listens to stories of how other people moved through difficult times themselves made me wonder:

- What is my self-talk? Do I use positive, encouraging words?
- What story am I telling myself (about me)?
- What am I allowing myself to learn about other people and situations?
- What can I learn from other people's stories?

We all have a story to share and it doesn't matter our age, our season, or our stage in life. We can learn from one another and grow in empathy and practical compassion along the way.

Chapter Eight

Setting a Social Foundation

*O*ne day I shared a link on social media about a specific topic addressed to a narrow slice of people on a noncontroversial (or so I thought) subject. I shared it in order to be helpful and had several people in mind who would benefit from the information. Their comments were positive and appreciative.

Then came an unexpected blast of cold air from an acquaintance in the form of a knee-jerk reaction. This person wrote a paragraph-long commentary about how wrong I was to share the information—the words and tone gave a feeling of being yelled at in person.

I made myself mentally and emotionally step back and not respond. I called a friend who knew this person, not to gossip but to process. I wanted the honest input I knew she would give. Was I wrong? Was the linked article indeed offensive?

I read her the article, then shared the response and asked for an honest opinion.

The response was, "No, it is not offensive or controversial at all, but if you have a certain situation going on, I can understand a negative response. However, that could certainly be worded differently. Like, 'Have you thought about this aspect of that situation? If not, let me offer a different perspective on it . . .'"

Social Kindness

Have you ever been completely misunderstood and met a harsh reaction? Or misunderstood something yourself and reacted before considering additional info? How often do we jump on with a post, comment, text, or email without stopping to think?

How do we view others? When we use our devices, do we think of human beings on the other side, or do we consider them part of the conglomerate of machinery and technology? Do we consider our word impact before we send something out? What if we took the time to consider a different point of view? Maybe if we stepped back just a moment, we could ask for clarification or even learn something new.

Our culture now encourages reactive people with a need to speak into everything without considering there are real people with authentic feelings and challenges on the other side of our posts, videos, or comments. It feels like any attempt at unity flew out the window and everyone dug trenches on their own "side," whatever that even means anymore.

We take our stance and dare someone else to dispute the words we share. We stand poised with our word darts, just looking for the next place to aim.

I've tried to think back and figure out where dismissive or rude communication began in recent years, and I can't determine the origin, and, really, it doesn't matter. Until we resolve to offer respect to everyone we encounter in person and online (whether we agree with them or not), nothing will change.

What if, instead, we offer a reasonable response that considers a situation from a different angle? When we recognize that we might need to nicely ask a question to get more information from someone else before we comment, or we remain open to offering more clarification for what we post, we help establish an open, agreeable environment to engage with other people.

What kind of interactive world could we have if we all strive to be reasonable and measured with our comments and responses to one another?

If we would all commit to respectful dialogue, we could live in a more harmonious world. I've heard people argue and place blame for the lack of civil discourse on groups or individuals, but really, spending time and energy on the origin doesn't engage us in helpful ways. We need to determine where we go from this point forward.

The open communication forum online offers wonderful opportunities to learn and share. It also provides space to hide behind devices. We can put out reactionary words with no pause or thought as to what they might trigger. They do nothing to help.

Even when someone is highly offensive, an angry response just inflames the situation. If something triggers a negative reaction, might we pause, take a moment, send a private message (if necessary) and say, "You might not know this aspect, just so you know . . ." If it is a stranger, determine if we really need to post or respond at all.

We've become a correcting society, ready and on edge to react or tell others how they're wrong. At the same time, we encourage people to tell and live their truth. But if we then jump on those same people, we cause a great imbalance, an unevenness between our words and actions. I want us to measure ourselves and to be reasonable. We don't have to correct each other all the time; we don't have to label; we don't have to throw inciteful, angry, mean words out there.

Kindness can infect our world for good. We're not respecting each other if the first thing we do is pile up. If it involves injustice or someone being harmed, then yes, we need to find a safe, healthy way to get the appropriate people involved. But what I'm addressing is general information or topics.

Just because someone doesn't believe exactly as we do doesn't mean we need to jump on them and say they're wrong for believing the way they do. If someone shares an article or thought with a snarky attitude, scroll on by.

I've learned that if I quickly move past harsh posts or comments, it can stop my anger or, at the very least, help me avoid wasting time on unnecessary emotion. Some people continually share stories or comment on things to justify their anger. If this is the case, I hide or mute their posts. If I see an ongoing pattern of insult, I quietly unfollow and maybe unfriend them. Every day that we allow those things into our brains, it revs up our system, we get stressed, and, really, we don't need any more of that, right?

For a post that proves troublesome or triggering, let's stop, take a day or two, and question the importance of a response. When we need to just move on, let's just move on. If we really feel strongly about respectfully offering a different perspective, then politely send a private message. Let's be the people who extend kindness to others and commit to putting better words and actions in the world. We are all different. Our Almighty Creator created us in his image with unique personalities, looks, cultures, environments, and interests.

If we are to ever hope for some kind of tranquil existence together, we must each take steps of positivity and encouragement.

This might even mean choosing to stay quiet and not comment on something just to have a retort. My mother always told me, "If you can't say something nice, don't say anything at all." There is such wisdom in what might seem like an old-fashioned, outdated idea.

When we offer a reasonable discussion on a topic (usually best accomplished in person in a one-on-one conversation with calm voices, surrounded with friendship, trust, and care), we can share our reasons why and offer new light on a particular topic.

One night, my friends Lisa and Scott invited me over for dinner. The table conversation took turns down every cultural side street you could imagine. We didn't wholeheartedly agree on several "hot topics," but we sat together and talked, offering our whys and hows. Not once were there edgy voices, harsh words, or any wounded feelings. We just enjoyed being together, having healthy conversation, a warm meal, and lots of laughter.

At the end of the evening, we talked about how remarkable it was to gather together, break bread, have robust conversation, and, as a result, feel even more affection and trust for one another. Oh, that we would all gather together and do the same! May we begin the change our culture so desperately needs.

Chapter Nine

A Healthy Mindset

*A*s we consider how our social lives integrate authentically with our personal lives, let's dig deeper into who we want to be and how we want to live out the sacred life we have here. This time and effort will prove to be a healthy self-investment.

Let's begin by evaluating a term often used to describe people with high levels of self-interest. We might discover areas within ourselves that could use a bit of remodeling to develop a higher sense of empathy and care for others.

A range represents the full spectrum of narcissism, and on *The Bearing Life® Podcast,* we learned a variety of behaviors that exemplify this very real disorder from my friend Dr. Les Carter.[14]

He illuminated the ways we can recognize narcissism and how to pay attention to our movement toward a narcissistic mindset when we become defensive or accusing and lure others into a non-productive pattern of communication.

We all display selfishness; it is human nature. Our selfish side shows up when we disregard someone else's needs, feelings, or perceptions because of our own agenda. It's also apparent when we want control and are inflexible or defensive. Each of us has our own degree and pattern of self-concern.

How can we have a healthy mindset and positive engagement with others? When we own selfish tendencies or behaviors and seek to become more selfless.

Healthy individuals choose to talk about the conflict and practice empathy, humility, patience, and self-restraint.

We can continue to move toward a healthy mindset by working on these things:

- **Be curious about others.** Narcissists want to just give advice or share their story while ignoring or minimizing the other person's situation. We need empathy, care, understanding, and patience with one another. Let's engage with others in their pain.
- **Encourage others to tell their story.** Even in the uncomfortable, awkward space, allow them to share.
- **Set good boundaries around relationships.** Know who you are, what you believe, and don't let others define you.

▼▼▼

A Closer Look: The Winds of Narcissism

Narcissism is a "hot" word to label people with whom we might not agree or to use against those we want to pierce with a fiery word dart. In reality, it actually refers to something much deeper. Dr. Carter offered his definition:

> "When we talk about narcissism, yes, we talk about a person who's self-enamored and they're just way

too into their own personal agenda. They have a high control need, and they're manipulative and exploitive, hence the gaslight movie. They want to be superior and have very low levels of empathy toward other individuals. It's like, 'I don't care what you feel, it's all about me,' and they operate with what I call alternate reality. They just kind of make up facts and truth that goes along with whatever their agenda requires. So, they're very difficult to engage with."[15]

Each of us experiences situations where we behave selfishly, desire control, and maybe act defensive. These come from our narcissistic bent. As healthy individuals, we will own it and acknowledge that, yes, I have these inclinations on occasion. I acknowledge the fact that I do and ask: What can I do to minimize or contain these? In other words, how are our interactions with others? Are we committed to our own agenda and control all the time, or are we just inclined? "We all have an inclination toward it; some have a deep, deep commitment to it."[16]

As Dr. Carter shared, narcissists have a deep commitment to pulling others into their world, their ways, their control, their overall authority. How do we counter this inclination in ourselves and prepare for unproductive interactions with others (those conversations that can lure us into this narcissistic bent)?

First, we commit to who we want to be and take time to define ourselves. Dr. Carter offered this key consideration for each of us, "Who do we want to be every day?"[17]

Second, we put self-definition and determination into practice. Sometimes we have fair warning ahead of time. Maybe we know we will see an argumentative co-worker or family member today.

When we know in advance, we can give ourselves that extra mental prep and go through that inner dialogue of who we want to be in those moments. More often, in the realities of life, we encounter people in a variety of ways every day. Maybe someone behaves rudely on a freeway, while ordering coffee at our favorite coffee bar, on social media, or in a store.

We don't know what happens in the backgrounds of other people's lives that lead them to have their own moments of frustration and anger, however inappropriately demonstrated. What we *can* control is who we are and how we respond.

Who do we want to be today (and every day)? We will probably have opportunities to react in ways we don't wish to. But if we spend the time to determine who we want to be and how we want to react and behave, we will intentionally begin to choose to offer dignity and respect. We will instinctively begin to maintain a calm interior and offer kindness to others, even when we might feel it is undeserved. It is called living out a life of grace. Not an easy feat, but a worthy, peaceful gift to give ourselves as well as offering it to others.

▲▲▲

Feeding Your Soul

My friend Melinda met me for lunch one day. At the time, I was on the lookout for co-working space with a modern vibe. We met at the restaurant she suggested and when we walked in, I developed an immediate crush on the place and decided to ask how they felt about people coming in to eat and then staying for a while to work.

Since the interior was small and only served breakfast and lunch, I wanted to be sensitive to their need to generate dollars versus my need to come in and take up a seat for a couple hours to work on my computer. I knew I would buy coffee and breakfast, but still, it was a new place and would probably become really popular and busy.

When we ordered, I asked the person behind the counter if it would be okay to come in a few days a week and hang out with my computer. He replied, "Hey, you do you. You do you." I got the gist of his meaning, but honestly, even that catchphrase has different meanings for different people. Part of me wanted to ask what he really meant by that, but I just smiled, said thanks, and we proceeded to eat our lunch.

I thought about that conversation a lot after we left. What does that mean, really?

We hear and say "you do you." What does it mean to me? To you? Do we even know ourselves? Some days I get so caught up in the busyness of life: I wake up, jump into my day. I don't stop, I don't plan. I don't think. I just prepare for my work and move on.

How often do I fail to think about what's feeding my soul? What's making me happy? What was I created for, and what does that look like?

We have so much in the way of technology and content that is designed to make us feel alive. But does it?

Are we too busy mindlessly swiping and scrolling and clicking to pay attention to our own existence? Do we ever dedicate the time needed to dig deep? Do we ever put our devices down and live our lives?

During a trip with some younger relatives, I had a stark reminder. I love photography and, being a creative, I wanted to capture beautiful images to have as reminders of the new lands we explored on our adventure.

One day, as I asked them to stop (for probably the twentieth time that day) so I could grab a pic of water or something, one of them turned to me and said, "You're missing half of what we're seeing right now because you're trying to capture the right moment instead of living in it."

Wow! Someone who grew up not remembering a time he didn't have a device in hand schooling me on not being in the moment.

It definitely got my attention.

His words made me ask myself, "Am I living this trip or am I just capturing it?" And I wasn't necessarily posting pictures that often; I just knew I wanted to look back later and revisit the places we'd seen and experienced.

But it made me think. Am I in the moment?

You and I were created to be unique individuals in our own lives. I find that when I get caught up looking at things on social media, I often fail to stay focused on my own work and sometimes get caught in the trap of comparison.

Then, my brain starts wandering down a negative path: "I don't look like that person," or "I don't have her clothes/makeup/house/ cooking talent," or "If I only had that outfit, how much better could I look and feel?"

When I know I'm dealing with disappointments, I seem to notice people who have all those things that I think I want at that moment. Then I find myself in a deprivation mindset, which, at the very least, robs me of contentment.

How much does "you do you" involve spending time and space to pay attention to *you*? Be mindful and intentional about knowing yourself well.

Knowing yourself well means paying attention to what makes your soul sing: familiarity with your interests and what you love to do. Are you making time and space in your life to do something that makes you feel alive? Is it art? Music? Reading? Being with a certain person? Being with family? Spending time with a pet? Investing time out in nature?

Consider how binge-watching has become a downer. How stressful is it to feel like we have to catch up on every episode of everything we want to watch or feel like we are missing out when we see posts about shows we haven't seen yet?

I have to ask myself, "Am I too distracted with content from other people or am I living my life and creating content for what I'm called to do and be?" Again, we all need to find our balance.

"You do you" is hard, isn't it? How do we know who we really are? Often, we need to involve others. Who knows you well enough to speak positively into your life and say, "Here's what I see in you..."

Do we have those people?

I have several core people who speak truth. They observe, engage, bring up, call me on, acknowledge, validate, and often correct. I don't hand that permission to them lightly. We have been through life experiences together that grow friendship exponentially. I know each of them wants the best for me—there is no competition, comparison, or jealousy. We really spur each other on.

What other ways can we take steps to balance our lives?

Healthier Choices

Some defining steps we can take:

- Examine our time-to-content ratio.
- Discover what makes our soul sing.
- Engage our community.
- Try something new.

Make time to explore something you've always wanted to learn, then go try it! If it ends up being something you don't love, that's okay—at least you tried. Anything we attempt can bring joy and satisfaction, even if only for a brief time.

What adds value to our lives and engages life with others, developing true friendships? Who are the core people in your life? If you don't have them, make it a goal to develop them. Or one.

Join a book club or Bible study. Get online with friends or sign up for activities in person. Check out social media groups for special interests or areas. The beauty of today's technology lies in its ability to help with initial connection. From there, we can meet, participate in life activities, and develop deeper layers of friendship.

Let's commit to mindfully engage in our lives. If all we do is sit and absorb everything that is available (and there is plenty to absorb), our lives stay on the thin surface of existence. I'm not saying don't spend time looking at content, but be mindful, be intentional, pay attention.

What are you listening to, watching, spending time on? Do you have reasonable time limits on these activities? How much time do you wish to devote?

The timing issue proves critical because setting limits on our content intake puts a really healthy boundary around it. Pick the things that will help you grow, encourage you, that are positive and inspiring. Set a time limit and once it is up, go engage in your life.

You go do you in a wonderful, amazing way!

I once took a step that brought much unexpected joy.

Jumping In

Several years ago, I knew I needed to engage creativity to counter a lot of left-brain work. I met and talked to an artist who said, "Give me eight hours of your time. In four lessons, I promise you will learn to draw."

I have to admit I laughed uncomfortably. Even quietly scoffed a bit, but I decided to leave my comfort zone and jump in.

I've spent a lifetime secretly envying my siblings' abilities to sketch and paint. In years past, the best I've been able to draw is a stick figure. I'm thankful for the creative abilities within me, but I always wanted to be able to capture visuals in simple pencil drawings.

My art teacher/new friend, Brenda, inspired me to try this creative outlet. She helped infuse a new layer of creativity into my world that would counter the underlying fear of failure.

She exuded positivity and encouragement. Her belief that I could accomplish my goal lit the fire within.

We jumped into the first lesson and I soon found myself wrapped up in the introductory drawing exercise. Before I knew it, two hours flew by. I left that day feeling great anticipation about where this would lead.

The second lesson, I showed up to find my model, the egg, sitting in the middle of my instructor's table. There was a mat and frame in front of the egg and my instructor invited me to sit and look at the light and shadow in order to capture its shape.

By the end of the lesson, I recreated my oval subject on the sketch paper. I couldn't believe I felt such an extraordinary sense of freedom and accomplishment.

Seemingly simple items and actions in life can significantly influence our confidence and contentedness. I not only drew the egg, but I also discovered a deeper sense of satisfaction and joy in doing so.

May I encourage you? Today, take a few minutes and sit quietly to ponder a new area of possibility and exploration in your world.

Jump out of your comfort zone, or just tiptoe. Determine to try something that will grow your creativity, increase your joy, or bring you to a place of peace and bravery. I may never be a Picasso, but I have come a long way from drawing simple stick figures.

Seek out people to help you. Reach out and explore new opportunities!

Chapter Ten

What About Your Wednesday?

O ne of my very close friends suffers from occasional panic attacks. During a conversation about all of her current stresses of life, she said, "My anxiety has been so high for so many months; it is a constant hum, an undercurrent that is ongoing." Her description resonated with me when I thought about that underlying life noise.

Not too long after our conversation, I recorded an episode of my podcast with Dr. Les Carter in which we talked about anxiety.[18] We all have anxious times in our lives: personal events, family, community, and national issues. With full 24/7 access to news and stories on social media, we can even experience unfolding anxiety in real time. I wanted to talk to Dr. Carter about how we can better understand and gain solutions to help manage anxiety in our lives.

He pointed out how the pandemic of 2020 revealed the reality of our vulnerability and how we need to offer grace to ourselves. "It is okay to say, I'm hurting, I'm struggling."[19]

Literal storms, all the layers of an ongoing worldwide pandemic, life issues, health, work ... overwhelming worries can keep our brains entangled in confusion and affect our basic life rhythms. What do we do when anxiety keeps us up at night?

Dr. Carter again encouraged us to give ourselves permission to admit when we need help, understand that we don't have answers for everything, and to accept that nights filled with stressful thoughts might just be nights when we don't experience a good sleep but can still rest. We need to pay attention and know ourselves: Seek help from wise friends, counselors, or doctors when needed, and remember we are humans who aren't meant to carry all the burdens of the world.

Dr. Carter said he listens for three components of anxiety when counseling clients: fear, anger, and control. When we feel controlled by or desire to control a situation, our anger can come out through frustration or irritability.

Wow, can I relate to that! Remember the massive tornado we talked about earlier? Well, the ongoing construction and equipment noise post-tornado for over two years resulted in lots of internal angst. Mentally, I found myself getting irritated and in a mindset of, "Can't this just be over?" Then I had to get my thinking back to, "Okay, it is what it is today. I must try to get back on track with remembering, 'Do what you have to do today. The racket of rebuilding structures continues, and for many moments, it feels eternal. Accept that this is reality right now and determine what you need to do in this day and move forward.'"

The difficult part is taking the time to stop for a minute to put it in perspective. Not only personal events but also world events can begin to affect our thinking and anxiety.

I often jump into wondering what's going to happen in my future. If I'm not careful with healthy mental boundaries, I start down the thought road of, "What does this pandemic mean for my life a year from now?" I can waste a lot of time and energy on imagining the worst and projecting into the future.

We can do the same with any overwhelming situation. I'm starting to learn how to better rein those thoughts in and tell myself, "I need to focus on today."

As Dr. Carter and I talked about control and fear, he offered a wise way to break down our thinking.

"Today is Wednesday, and I have my Wednesday to get through. I need to figure out what I'm going to do with my Wednesday. So, I am going to try to have control in the long run in such a way that I know where I'm going, and I have a game plan that I will execute. But in the event that there are just some things that I can't really maneuver, I simply need to think about what I am going to do today."[20]

Honestly, when he shared this Wednesday thought, I physically felt my mental and emotional burdens ease; it just felt reasonable and manageable.

We then broke it down further and talked about putting the situation into a more workable amount. What can we control? It depends on many variables, but I want to encourage you to consider what you can do about it in the next day, hour, or even five-minute increments. Depending on the severity of the out-of-control feeling, smaller chunks of management could be more peaceful.

One of the helpful ways he guided listeners to consider anxiety-laden control was in the context of external versus internal. We can't control another person, responses, or situations, but we can control how we react.

Let's ask ourselves, who do we want to be? Do we want to be people who respond with patience and decency? We can choose to respond with the same rudeness just thrown at us, or we can be confident in the people we are (respectful, kind) and react with healthy boundaries that reflect our desired selves to others.

As we mindfully manage small interactions each day, we establish a pattern of response within ourselves that maintains calm confidence. If we know who we are and have goals about who we want to be with others, then we can resolve much of the anxiety about the unknowns of our life and future.

Pandemic-Related Anxiety

Because of the global pandemic, I've heard many stories of worry, stress, and grief both online and through conversations with friends.

In normal circumstances, each of us walks through varying seasons of worry throughout our lives. But the time following a pandemic brings a multitude of issues that can overwhelm even the most optimistic and hope-filled among us.

So. Many. Issues.

Including how to make wise decisions about . . .

- When to gather with others.
- How to stay healthy.
- Making home and work-life balance work for you.
- Juggling schedules and tasks of everyone in your home.
- Engaging with others if you live alone.

For many, the list of potential stresses goes on and on. We can counter these gusts of stress by doing a little work on our individual selves—who we want to be and how we want to live.

A Closer Look: The Winds of Depression

There is no doubt the stress and isolation of a worldwide pandemic affected most people in some way. Experts believe we have witnessed a mental health epidemic as many Americans (and people worldwide) have found themselves battling symptoms of anxiety and depression.[21]

I've known my friend Ann for years and had no idea she walked with depression. It's not that she covers it up, but that I had never seen signs of her struggle. I've watched someone who lives an incredible life. She found her passion and vocation, loves her family, loves people, life, and God. If you or anyone you know stands in a dark place of "I don't know how I can climb out of this," I'd like to encourage you! I know someone who has been there, and she's moved forward in healthy, vibrant ways. When I heard her tell some of her story, I asked her to join me on my podcast and share it with my listeners.

> "It's taken a lot of work and a lot of medication and a lot of therapy for me to be the person that you see. This takes courage. It takes way more courage to seek help for depression than it does to act like nothing is wrong. A coward does that. You pick up your mat and you walk and you go find someone. Check it out, get recommendations, search the web, all that. You find a doctor that you trust. Maybe even start with your general practitioner or women with your OBGYN—who, I guarantee you, hears this story every day. But you have to take the first step toward your healing."[22]

Bravery doesn't mean that we have everything figured out. Courage comes when you take steps for your mental health so that you can become like my friend Ann and live a vibrant life.

Ann further walked through a description of determining a diagnosis and finding the right treatment. She shared about the lengthy process required to implement the right combination for each individual. It is a journey!

The diagnosis and treatment are not the only necessary ingredients needed to work through the darkness of depression. Find someone with whom you can process your feelings; have a friend you can talk to and share your heart and offer the same in return. Some helpful active listening tips Ann offered included maintaining eye contact, facing the person, listening without judgment, giving feedback (without words) so they know you're listening, and occasionally asking clarifying questions.

When we talked about practical ways we can walk through depression (and really, any challenging obstacle), Ann shared that we are responsible for what we can control about our happiness, and we must take ownership. She realized it was her job to make sure she got better.

We have to pay attention to ourselves, be responsible for our behaviors to the best of our ability, and learn when we need help and when our bodies are off. We need trusted friends that we can ask, "Hey, have you noticed _____ going on with me?" As we share our stories, we feel empowered to act, and we also inspire others in their own life story.

Chapter Eleven

Living Your Story

*O*ften, opportunities to try new things come in unexpected ways. One thing I never thought I'd try was podcasting. One day, out of the blue, my great-nephew Jeremy said, "Aunt Julie, you should do a podcast." I said, "No, I don't think that's for me."

It then became a game because every time I talked to him, he would say, "Hey, have you thought about that podcast?" Every time, I said no.

Then I found myself having coffee with Vanessa, a new, younger friend I met when I served with a nonprofit organization. As we talked about our jobs and work, she asked about my speaking and writing and then said, "You really should do a podcast."

I said no.

Now I'm doing a podcast and love it. I'm embracing it. My goal with the show is to discuss real life and learn helpful ways we can navigate different situations and offer practical compassion to one another.

The name of the podcast is *The Bearing Life® Podcast*. It is a twist not only on my life but also the lives we are called to live together. I couldn't bear children, we are called to bear fruit (find and live purpose, fulfillment), we are called to love one another, and that includes helping others bear their burdens.

Life can be hard, and we need each other for support to get out from under burdens, move through them, and avoid getting stuck. Sometimes we spend a little extra time spinning our wheels, but we don't have to stay there. People and actions are what help us in the aftermath of storms. We can bear our burdens well, come alongside others, and help them bear theirs in turn. As we then move forward, we bear fruit within our lives.

We have a life mountain range to traverse and our travels include up, down, and even sideways detours, as well as moments that are on path and off path, with gorgeous views from the highest peaks. Some life seasons will encompass wonderful growing times in the valley or wilderness. We are running a long-term race.

I don't want to take up space; I want to contribute value to life. Through the podcast, I talk to others, hear their stories, listen to how they dealt with their lives, and share these conversations with you. They are filled with positivity and thankfulness.

As we try new things and walk through open doors, we must focus on our own opportunities, taking great care not to compare ourselves to others.

The Comparison Enemy

One day, I shared with my friend Kyla how I felt about the comparison struggle on social media. During the conversation, I expressed sadness for younger women who voiced similar struggles with me. Kyla and I talked about how difficult it can feel when we start down the comparison road. We agreed that it seemed easy to merge into the traffic of that particular insecurity when viewing posts and stories and being reminded of an area in our lives that we perceive as lacking.

Not too long after that discussion, she called to tell me about her longtime friend "Mary." They'd met years before in high school, not really close, but they liked to touch base occasionally to get updates on life events.

She hadn't seen Mary post on social media for a while. She contacted her and found out that Mary had left social media because her "life had fallen apart" and she felt like "everyone else's life looked so perfect." If a mature, seasoned woman who had walked through a lot of life felt this way, what must younger men and women feel like who haven't yet lived through life circumstances that can lead to greater inner confidence and better equip them to handle disappointments?

We all have challenges. Does your default pattern on social media resemble "I only want to post the best pictures and give the impression that my life is all together?"

There is nothing wrong with sharing joyous life events and good news or desiring to look great in pictures. However, if we only post "the best" of ourselves, we all falsely believe that "everyone else has it all together and my life stinks." Or we fear "if anyone really knew what a mess my life looks like right now . . ."

No one has a perfect life. Not one of us has it all together all the time. (Don't even get me started on the variety of filters that I must admit have made me envious of someone else's looks on many occasions!)

Just proceed and scroll with caution. Remember to put your own mental filter in place and view things through the lens of knowing that each person probably put a lot of time into presenting the best of themselves. If we could all put just a smidge more authenticity out there, we might feel more understood and less like an outsider.

We can also compare our suffering with the "they don't understand because they haven't been through my situation" filter that can skew our empathy.

As my friend and mentor Dr. Sandra Glahn says, "Be careful with playing the suffering Olympics." Once, someone said to me, "You might not have had a biological baby, and I know that was hard, but mine is harder . . . my child, who was an honors student in high school and college, is now a drug addict." We each have our own history, struggle, and pain. We cannot fully know the experience of someone else, and we better serve one another when we don't compare our suffering.

Comparison can divert us to the land of jealousy, envy, or even entitlement. Let's look through the frame of encouragement or admiration for the other person's joy or accomplishment and move forward in our own confidence and authentic life. Remember, comparison is not our friend, and we're all in some variation of struggle, or we've just come through one. We can see beyond the façade and seek to joyfully live in the now, appreciating where someone else succeeds and move on to strive ahead in our own lives.

Keeping Your Story

When I was a senior in college, my sorority officers asked parents to send a letter to their senior daughter as a surprise. Each week during our meeting, they read several letters. I still have this handwritten treasure my parents wrote about how special our family and life were with me as their child and their pride in the person I was becoming.

Think of someone special in your life to handwrite (yes!) and mail a letter. Maybe your young adult child or a letter to a sibling, former teacher, or neighbor. Words of affirmation, telling someone the amazing, incredible things you see in them can add a wonderful layer of self-knowledge, confidence, and positive impact to their life.

You are the keeper of your story.

You hold your story and share it to help others with their perspective of similar events, memories, and family history. When we share stories, we learn about one another's highs and lows, joys and heartaches.

We can also develop deeper bonds with others in our communities. Our willingness to share tales of joy and compassion offers encouragement to strangers. We realize that we are not alone in our wonder or grief.

Instead of storms taking over our lives, let's learn what we can, manage the aftermath, and face the horizon with hope.

Chapter Twelve

Know Your Value

*T*he influence of social media can provide an underlying current of perfection that often alters our self-perception and value. In our world of input from "perfect posts," we must intentionally refresh ourselves and others with healthy, positive messages of our worth.

In recent conversations with a variety of people, the question of "Am I enough?" comes out in large and small ways. Don't we all wonder about that at different times in our lives?

It's time to switch up our mindset!

Made in the image of God, *imago Dei* means I am of great value, and I am enough. You are enough. This doesn't mean we stop striving for good or living with excellence. Rather, it means knowing that at the heart of it all, made in the image of Almighty God, we are enough; we are unique creations lovingly made for this time and place.

I can get distracted by the attention-getting noise that shouts at us, trying to sell us something to improve ourselves, our relationships, our lives. Some of the messages represent necessaries we need to enhance our existence; some just seem to be sparkly distractions in the life dust that blows around us. I must intentionally stop to remind myself that my *being* is of great value to God, and if I believe what he creates holds great value, then I not only need to believe it about myself but also believe it about all people.

Sometimes it is difficult to completely accept—I can struggle to truly believe my own worth and avoid listening to the negative tapes within. Often, I need to remind myself that I am capable and worthy because God created me, gifted me, and continues to work in me every day. The more I embrace this truth, the less I allow detrimental thoughts to impact my actions and decisions (or lack thereof).

In today's world with such divisive words and actions, I also need to remember that I must hold the same belief about other people's worth, even when I think they might be putting harmful negativity and harshness out into the world. I've had to learn to pause, take a step back, and not let myself have an internal, emotional reaction to someone I might not even know.

Looking back on my tornado experience offers a chance to see how events in life unfolded and presented incredible opportunities. I couldn't begin to see those in the first hours, days, and even weeks, but as I look back on that time, I can clearly see such good that came out of it.

Yes, the storm brought destruction and fear. It also ushered in an amazing opportunity to witness people valuing strangers, so much so that they ran into the destruction to help save, find, and lead them to safety. Others helped clean up, repair, remodel, and rebuild.

During the chaotic aftermath of almost constant mechanical sounds of chain saws and nail guns, neighbors pulled together as builders: of help, support, care, and relationships.

Life storms, literal and figurative, offer us an opportunity to be builders. Here are a few ways to consider how we spend our time and presence on Earth. We don't have to do them all at once. Dedicate about fifteen minutes each week to consider one question. Do them at your own pace.

- Who do you want to be?
- Who are you on social media? How do you want to be known on social media or through in-person relationships?
- What does your communication sound like to others? What do your actions say?
- What are the big life goals you want to achieve?
- What is your desired destination?

Kindness and practical compassion cost us nothing and could give others the world. When we take time to live out a ready-as-much-as-we-can-be life, we exhibit these habits to those around us and inspire them to do the same.

Think of someone in your life who is younger and for whom you wish to set a good example.

This could be a family member, neighbor, co-worker, or maybe even someone following you on social media.

They are watching, even if you don't realize it. They pick up on your tone, facial expressions, and actions.

How do you want to influence those coming along behind you?

When you walk through difficult times or take really brave steps, a variety of people will watch to see how you handle your journey. Maybe they are in a similar situation and are quiet about it or are staying isolated and need the encouragement to take the next baby step in life.

Watching an athlete in the 2021 Summer Olympic Games impressed me for many reasons and also made me compare the situation to how we can sometimes feel in life.

Simone Biles, an amazing, talented, "greatest of all time" gymnast, proved her humanity. The burden on her to succeed felt overwhelming even to me as I watched the media build-up and the on-camera commentators discussing expectations for Team USA and Simone Biles, in particular.

Then she faced her own storm right in the middle of the games. She unexpectedly developed the "twisties."[23] Gymnasts who commented expressed familiarity with the term and situation, describing the unnerving uncertainty experienced when a gymnast attempts to execute a routine on one of the apparatus and gets "lost in the air." Simone Biles gave this description:

> "You literally cannot tell up from down. It's the craziest feeling ever, not having an inch of control over your body. What's even scarier is since I have no idea where I am in the air, I also have NO idea how I'm going to land or what I'm going to land on. Head/hands/feet/back . . ."[24]

It filled my heart with gratitude to hear the immediate responses from fellow gymnasts when Simone Biles stepped back from competing to evaluate her ongoing participation. The announcers explained it well and offered empathy for her. Social media became filled with posts and articles, and the ones that proved helpful were from other gymnasts who related similar "twisties" stories. They offered their understanding and helped convey information to a watching world that didn't have a clue about this physical and mental challenge.

I honestly cannot imagine how terrifying the situation must have felt for her. A betrayal by the body you've trained for years unexpectedly occurring as you're poised on the world stage for a huge spotlight competition. I was so impressed with her determination to do the right thing for herself and her team. The gathering-together teamwork and support they offered one another are well worth a close study to utilize in our own life teams!

Thinking about the "twisties" gives us an understanding of our emotional fallout during uncomfortable or traumatic events.

We might experience a similar disconnect or inability to gain sure footing in the middle of fierce winds, or maybe we see someone else in our midst appearing to struggle with uncertainty. Whatever we walk through, however we overcome, all the ways we persist and seek to live with excellence, can inspire those around us and even beyond. They all contribute to a legacy of love and the care we model and leave for others.

A Lasting Legacy

I don't know why I hadn't seen it before, but one day I noticed a heart carved in the trunk of a small Aspen tree growing right beside my deck. I was fascinated. I wondered who carved it and why. I knew a little about the former homeowner, but she had long since passed on and there was no one to ask. So, my story mind created lots of different scenarios about the who and why of this sign of affection.

I love good love stories—in songs, movies, books, or real life! They give me hope for a future one of my own, they encourage all of us in our struggles, they inspire us in our dedication to living a legacy of love through family, friends, and community.

The story[25] that Dr. Willie O. Peterson, my friend and mentor, tells about his parents gives me hope. If you have a troubled family background or feel the isolation and loneliness of unexpected events, grab onto the beauty of his parents, their example, and family.

He previously shared with me a little of his family background and what an incredible legacy his parents left him and his siblings. The trials and tribulations of both their lives led to dedication to and love for one another and their own family. They had a beautiful story of overcoming, bearing life burdens well, and bearing incredible fruit through their family and beyond.

Dr. Peterson's parents overcame the storms of adversity to build a strong family. After difficult starts in life and unpleasant childhoods, they committed to raising a connected family. They saturated their lives and children with faith, knowledge, love, and promises of God. Dr. Peterson and his siblings realize the legacy their parents left them and have passed it on to their own families. He and his brothers fondly recall saying they "wanted to marry a woman like Mom, so they could show her they loved her like Dad loved Mom." Dr. Peterson's father continued to love and serve his mother until his last day on Earth.

Both parents modeled the love of God—in their marriage, to their children, and in their community. Even though they each began life in a dark place, after meeting Jesus Christ, their lives and the lives of all who met them were transformed by his light and love.

Their story offers great inspiration for all to leave a lasting legacy.

My heart tree offered a legacy, but not in the way I originally imagined. Disease took over several surrounding trees, and the time came when it could no longer stand. Before it was taken down, I captured a picture of the heart carved in the trunk to remind me of possibilities—stories of love, home, and a hopeful future.

The tree company saved that section of trunk for me but, after a while, even that couldn't be preserved. So, I look at the picture and think fondly of that tree. It also reminds me that we have opportunities to build into the lasting love legacy we pass on to the people in our lives.

We don't have to wait for the "right person" to give our love; we can love others well in our family and friend circle. We can offer love through compassion, dignity, respect, and service in our community and even online. We can build into a legacy of love that continues on and on and on when we love God and love one another.

Our healthy forward momentum in the aftermath of a storm or in the face of an uncertain future can help transform someone else's challenge. Our brave steps can inspire another when we live with a willing attitude to share and reach out to those around us.

Living Authentically

When we know how a variation of a weather front or disaster feels, when we determine who we are in the midst of it and have an idea of what tools can help, then we are better able to step in and show compassion and empathy for others.

Maybe they are drowning in emotion and need someone like you or me to show a general road map to find their way out of their situation. We don't always know when someone is looking to us for how to do something—not just the steps to accomplish a task, but how to "do life."

People are crying out for authenticity, especially in the church where we feel such pressure to do life well or to look like we've got it all together and have no problems. We all start as sinners in need of a savior, and somewhere along the way, we morph into trying to look as if we have the perfect life, almost pridefully like we don't want to appear in need of any help.

We can seek to be "good" Christians who do everything the "right" way, but there lies the lie coated with unhelpful motivation. The truth? Not one of us is good without the Lord, and no one is perfect. No one can relate to someone pretending to have it all together—no one. Our witness to God's work in our lives collapses when we attempt to present a false front!

We *don't* need to stand up in front of the crowd and spew our problems all over everyone. In an age where people are hungry for life-changing truth and hope, we must be willing to balance sharing our struggles with showing our God who sees us through.

We *do* need to be mindful of how we present ourselves, in person and on social media. In an age of perfection-promoting social media filters that evoke extreme comparison, we must learn to be real with rich authenticity in our lives.

Again, they are watching, those hungry for understanding, empathy, validation, and the need to feel not alone. They desperately need to see they are not the only ones who know fear and failure.

Please, remember that you are not alone in life—you're seen by others. We need each other for so many reasons.

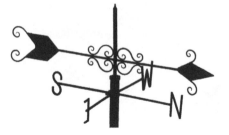

Part Two

Rebuilding or Reinforcing Community

Chapter Thirteen

Connecting Steps

*W*e all want our lives to mean something, to make a difference somewhere, to know that we are seen and that our presence matters. The good news? You are relevant. You can make a difference. You can have incredible impact for good, each and every day.

The better news? It's up to you! You choose to live your relevance. Every. Single. Day.

We commit to simply smile at a cashier in the grocery store, not bury ourselves in our devices but engage with the people who help us. Let's notice them and help them feel seen and valued. Say good morning, ask how their day is going, and thank them for their help. Say have a good day as we walk off.

Have you ever wondered how many people go through their line and never even look at them or speak to them? How they might feel like they are just the equipment or machinery necessary to get things done for others because they aren't seen by the people right in front of them? Throughout the pandemic, I committed to really engaging with people who are vital to our daily life, especially while wearing a mask.

As I went through checkout lines, I can't even tell you how many of them had a look of shock that someone was talking to them instead of focusing on their phone.

I started asking how they were doing, commiserating about our common weariness of the pandemic. Then I began asking about their experiences with customers and that I was hopeful people came through the line and expressed thanks. Wow, was I wrong! I've now lost count of how often I've said, "I'm so sorry" for the treatment they received from strangers. We all need to know we matter and are worth someone else's time and polite conversation.

Another choice that can make a difference? Take a few minutes and call someone older than you to just check in, ask how they're doing, and listen. Offer them the presence of your time during what might be a lonely, long day.

Invest action in someone younger who needs a caring, healthy older person to listen.

Your life matters.

You don't need an online platform or a large following or to look perfect in order to make a difference in the world around you.

Your words matter.

Your encouraging posts matter. You never know who is watching and reading and how it can impact them.

Making Each Moment Count

What if we develop a mindset of greeting each day as a once-in-a-lifetime experience? In fact, it really is, if you think about it.

You are trading this day of existence—for what? What will you exchange for this precious time today? You will never have this day again. We always want something of value for what we give. We pay money to receive services and, if they aren't up to our expectations, we give the company a low rating or bad review. When we go to a restaurant, we exchange dollars for food.

You have this day, this moment.

What will you give, and what would you like to achieve? It doesn't have to be perfect or large in scope; it can be something as simple as wanting to give someone a smile or joy or hope today.

I've struggled in the past with perfectionism, and, to be honest, I still do occasionally. The more time I invest, the bigger difference I want to make. Or, the more impact I seek to have, the bigger the temptation to freeze because I fear not doing the job perfectly—even when my head knows that no one is perfect and no task can truly be done to perfection.

So, I must stop and remind myself to approach the job with excellence, not perfection. I've had to train my focus on doing my best in everything large and small and to give priority to intangibles like compassion, kindness, and respect toward others.

Can you relate?

Remember, we can change a life simply by looking someone in the eye and saying good morning, in showing a stranger that somebody sees them. It doesn't cost anything but a little intention.

- Who or what led you to make new, creative discoveries in your life?
- How did they do this?
- Are you still pursuing them, or do you need to try again?
- Whom can you inspire to pursue their dreams? Reach out this week and schedule some time together.

Connection and Community

My Texas roots run deep! My dad grew up in the country where his large family picked cotton, while my mom lived out her childhood and youth in the big city.

My parents spent all of their married life in Dallas. For years we also had a farm in the country; I am grateful to have the experience of both worlds. Our parents taught us about building community with those in our neighborhood, friends, church, city, and even on vacations. My mom modeled the value of caring connections throughout life. She still exchanges Christmas cards with people (some in other countries) she met on different trips.

My two siblings and I were raised in the church firmly grounded in the truth of Jesus Christ. Having the foundation of church community proved important not only for how we were raised and the lifelong friendships from that time but also in developing the internal community each of us began with God.

Three unexpected turns in life hugely influenced my adult years and opened up new opportunities for connection and community development.

The first major turn happened in my thirties. I was single and had a great job involving a lot of business travel. A mission trip to Uganda with a singles group from church changed my life. For the first time, I realized that a faith-filled, fruitful life in Christ needed continual relationship connection and growth, not kept to the sidelines of life until I needed him. My community of friends at church and the bonding experience of travel in an incredible new environment established roots with several friendships that continue to inform and influence my life in a powerful way.

Several years later, the second turn arrived. The unexpected turn of infertility led me to seminary, where I earned two degrees and discovered an entirely new path in life and relationships. The barrenness of infertility helped me discover ways to mentor and coach, to write, teach, and speak, to better understand the responsibility we all have to spiritually mother, mentor, parent and show up in others' lives.

The third unexpected turn in life was the disintegration of a seventeen-year marriage (over a long period of time), which led to a new layer of understanding in my heart about equipping others to offer practical compassion in areas of pain and challenge in our lives.

My divorce deepened my trust and faith in God. It broadened my understanding of the experiences that God allows in order to better love people and him in the most challenging places. It reminded me that we could find many ways to develop our community of people through different seasons and varying layers of connection.

I treasure opportunities to build community—coming together to strengthen relationships, fellowship, meet new friends, and bond with those already formed.

Time together, set apart for God, growth, and our friendships is so important yet difficult to justify in our list-filled, responsibility-driven lives.

Now, let's spend some time building community.

▼▼▼

A Closer Look: The Winds of Loneliness

Annie joined me on the podcast for an episode about Valentine's Day.[26] Even though the episode offered season-specific information for singles, we can incorporate Annie's suggestions in a variety of moments when we feel lonely and need to gather our friends.

You see, Annie found herself facing Valentine's Day as a single and knew she needed to make a plan. She decided to invite other friends over to cook, drink wine, and spend time together. As she put it, "I needed to take responsibility and put myself out there. Sometimes I have moments of sitting home and saying, 'This sucks,' but I try most of the time to stay busy and get out there doing things instead of staying home and saying, 'Woe is me.'"[27]

I applaud her resolve. Often it can be easier to just wait for someone else to plan and invite—or sit home alone. But she took the chance and began texting friends to see who wanted to join in.

She has a gift for hospitality and also a passion for food, and she used both to bring friends together for a fun night of food, hanging out together, sharing stories, and lots of laughter.

Dig deep and find that willingness to invite others into your home. Reach out, make a plan, be awkward.

We often wait for someone else to do the planning or reaching out, but if all of us feel insecure and wait for another to act, guess what? We could find ourselves sitting alone while waiting for someone else to take action.

Everyone has some kind of struggle. Let's decide to face our inner awkward teen and text a friend (or several) and invite them! If you enjoy cooking, offer to cook or ask each person to bring something. Maybe just order pizza. Enjoy conversation and catch up, play board games, share joy and laughs together. Truly engage with each other for an evening.

Food, conversation, laughter, and stories build layers of bonding and friendship. The more time we spend together, the deeper the sense of community we develop.

That phone call or text just might be the beginning of a meaningful community group of friends.

Who Surrounds You?

"Dime con quién andas, y te diré quién eres." I learned this wise Spanish proverb on a business trip many years ago. The translation given to me: "Tell me who you walk with, and I'll tell you who you are." Another saying in life: Birds of a feather flock together.

We become more like who we hang out with, follow, and read. This doesn't mean we aren't unique; we just need to be careful with the balance of intake. Negative people often shape negativity in us.

All kinds of people in our lives speak into our journey; however, make sure your *inner* circle, those close influencers you know personally (who invest in your life with their time and action, and you into theirs), make sure these people speak loving truth into your existence.

Don't let negative voices rob you of the opportunity to do or try what you feel called to do. Be very careful what you allow to take up space in your head and influence your behaviors and goals.

Long ago, I studied acting and on the final day of the last class I took, the teacher (a successful actor) gave individual advice about each person's potential in the biz. Over the course of the class, he gave me positive, glowing feedback. During his class wrap-up, I waited in anticipation to hear his "declaration" over what I should pursue. As he worked his way around the circle of students, giving specific input, I was the last one he addressed.

I held my breath, waiting to hear profound words of encouragement and direction. It felt as if my very future hinged on the pearls of wisdom and guidance he was about to impart . . .

"Julie, if you don't stay in this business, you are a horse's ass." That is all he said.

He then turned and addressed the class with concluding words. I sat, astounded and deflated.

It was the last acting class I took. Ever.

I can look back now and evaluate my talent and his meaning in the whole picture of the critiques and feedback he gave me at the time. Those last words he meant as encouragement to stay in the business and keep pursuing my dreams.

Unfortunately, in my insecurity, all I heard was, "You aren't good enough. You'd be a fool." I also had a few other voices speaking negatively into this dream of mine. In spite of their opinions, I knew the professional actor/teacher thought I had the talent, but at a crucial point, I misinterpreted his meaning, and guess what I did? I walked away from something I enjoyed. I loved the entire acting process—on camera, development, camera angle, lighting, watching all the people involved and doing their tasks. I wasn't seeking self-glorification; I felt alive and like an effective communicator, part of a creative team.

Please hear me. I. Walked. Away.

Because of other people.

I've accepted it, and even though I now have similar creative work and pursuits, I have thought, "What would my life look like if I had just . . ."

Your life is not about *them*. With respect, you have this one life to explore, adventure, and architect. Invite and consider input from those you trust, but as an adult, your life is your own.

Consider where your talents lie. Gather honest feedback from people you trust and, when you know that you have the talent and desire to pursue a direction, move forward. Though the winds of negativity may blow, dig deep and engage the right people for *you*, and follow your God-given dreams.

Much later in life, as I followed a new dream, a beautiful circle of friends came together in support and practical care to ensure that I succeeded where God was calling me.

The Support of Friends

I stared in disbelief at the seven-foot-tall, 600-pound metal storage unit on top of my left foot.

Twenty seconds before, as I pushed the cabinet on wheels, it suddenly tilted in slow motion and slammed down on my foot. Ten minutes later, I entered the emergency room of a hospital a few blocks away. The on-call emergency doctor told me the three middle bones in my foot were broken and I had major tissue damage (so much weight hit my foot that the trauma literally killed part of the flesh!).

I left the ER on crutches with a massive boot on my leg and a dire warning to put *no* weight or pressure on that foot overnight before heading straight to an orthopedic surgeon the next day.

The next morning, I was told that the broken bones were in alignment, and if I could avoid putting *any* weight on my foot for nine weeks, I *might* not need surgery.

My foot and ankle were so swollen I required a wheelchair with a leg extender to keep my foot constantly elevated. Any time I lowered it below my knee, I suffered excruciating pain.

With three weeks left in my very first semester of graduate school, I did not know how I would continue my studies.

I felt defeated.

"Lord, you called me to go back to school, and now there is no way for me to complete this semester."

Four of my closest friends knew about my situation and came up with a plan. Dorothy, Jacque, and Suzanne reviewed the days

I drove to school and divided up my schedule: Each one took on one day a week to drive me to school, wheel me to class, wait outside, wheel me back to the car, and drive back home. These were women with families, jobs, and busy church and community involvement.

The fourth friend, Kyla, took me on weekly trips to the grocery store and other errands.

These friends faithfully came alongside, committed to helping me finish that semester. They held me up, nourished me, provided transportation, encouraged me, and loved me well.

They were truly the hands and feet of Jesus living out his instruction in John 15:12–13, "This is my commandment, that you love one another, just as I have loved you. Greater love has no one than this, that one lay down his life for his friends."

These friends laid down their lives, their regular schedules, duties, and comfort to see me through.

It was a stunning example of fellowship, love, and community.

Our close friends and loved ones make up part of our community, and those in the larger circles of our lives do too. Neighbors, co-workers, church members, committee members, school volunteers, and treasured friends from childhood compose a few of the layers of community in life.

A Closer Look: The Winds of Mental Health

Michelle and Mike, married for thirty-five years, entered a mental health crisis seven years into their marriage. Mike suffered a concussion in a car accident that seemed to trigger a change in his mental health. As Michelle explained, he left work one day to go to lunch and see about a car check-up. After his accident that day, he never went back to work.

Their lives literally changed in the space of a few hours.

> "We looked at it as an illness from the beginning. This is nothing Mike did to himself. He didn't cause this to happen, so let's discover how to live in this as best we can. All these years, it sounds like no problem, like click your fingers, and we lived through it. It was painful then, and there was a lot of discovery that we needed to do. First of all, there were lots of doctor visits to get an appropriate diagnosis."[28]

They found themselves in a new church community, feeling a little isolated and wondering how to live out this up and down time of the unfamiliar storm. "God put me in touch with the right people that I needed for that time. So, I had fewer relationships, but they were just the right relationships."[29]

They found support through the medical teams and their community. As Michelle emphasized, not only did Mike need care from the community, but she did as well. Sometimes in difficult events, especially long-term situations, the caregivers feel isolated and in need of their own support.

> "You know, when you're dealing with mental health issues, you've got one person that's going to doctors and getting treatment, maybe going to counselors and getting therapy. Then you've got family members— who is taking care of them? So, in our situation, I had people who cared about what was happening to me

and who actually had some experience. They helped to walk with me through this journey while Mike was getting the care he needed."[30]

Sometimes our pain keeps us from reaching out to others. Maybe we sit in confusion, raw grief, frustration, or just not even knowing how to communicate all the things swirling around in those moments. When we reach out to ask someone to walk with us and courageously share, we can help one another. I love how Michelle shared her personal encouragement for those in a crisis. "When we live in fear of revealing what's really going on with us, we're allowing the evil one to have control of the situation when God wants to get the glory. We didn't understand what was happening, but I wasn't afraid of talking about it."[31]

How do we walk well with people in the midst of a mental health struggle? We pray, show up, and listen. Let them talk and process without trying to fix it. This journey belongs to them, but we can come alongside and remind them they are not alone. They have us, community, maybe their family if close by, and most of all, God.

Circles of Community

The larger, more general circles of community make up the outer aspects of our lives: people in our city, broader faith communities, neighbors, friends from different seasons of life, and online community. These are the people with whom we have limited connection and minimal engagement.

Think through your general community. Who adds to your personal root system?

A couple of years ago, I went to a Christmas party and saw several friends from childhood and high school. As I stood talking with one of them about how great it was to stay in touch through social media and how special our memories felt, I commented that I didn't understand why, but even though lots of life and miles separated all of us, we still shared such a strong bond.

He replied, "That's because we knew each other 'when.'" It immediately made sense. When we stay in touch with those who knew us "when," we feel a comfort and knowingness that others won't understand. We knew one another's childhood homes, nicknames, siblings, teen crushes, and awkward high school wardrobe choices. There is something really special about being known, especially by those who can take a stroll down memory lane with us.

Your Foundational Circles

I've found there are seven foundational circles needed in life. The number of people in each depends on individual circumstances and desires: family, significant other, core friends, stormy friends, mentors, God, and myself (yes, we are in community with ourselves!).

Go through your necessary people. Here are some key folks I consider helpful in my life:

Family: My family consists of my parents and siblings and then a large extended family. I also include friends who are like family in this circle.

Significant other: If you have a significant other in your life, you have a crucial role in one another's lives. Part of commitment lies in the ability to hold one another up, communicate in healthy ways, share the good times, and provide a shoulder of support during the challenging times. Walk with care because the swirl of winds can draw us closer or drive a wedge between us. Seek outside wisdom of close friends, mentors, or counselors when additional help is needed.

Core friends: I have a variety of friends from different areas and times in life. Those I hold particularly close are the five absolute truth tellers who love and challenge me, ask key questions, check in, and pray for me. They add intrinsic value and depth to my friend community.

Knowing that they want the best for me gives emotional security, so I'm free to give them permission to speak honestly into my life. If they see something I'm doing (negative or positive), often one will say, why are you doing *that*? Or why are you spending time on *this*? Key questions from them offer me opportunities to take a closer look at my choices, direction, and action in life decisions or tasks. This can help give me personal clarity and also offer a chance to run ideas by them to get their perspective (maintaining a healthy balance/boundary all the while!).

One of these friends proved instrumental when I walked through several years of an infertility storm. She would occasionally say, "Okay, I get it; I know you're still mourning this loss of a dream, but you've been mourning for a while and now seem stuck. I understand that you have ongoing grief, but I want to know what you plan to do about that area over there? You still have a life. What are you doing today about other purposes that *are* realities in your world?" It would often snap me out of the mournful fog and make me truly consider where and how I needed to take a step and move forward.

A caution: First, she was a trusted friend and confidant. Second, she only made comments like this after a long time of watching me mourn the loss of my dream. Third, she never told me not to take time to grieve every layer.

There were times when I had to push back a little and say, "You know, you've never experienced this. So, for this particular pain, it's going to take me a minute (or a multitude of them) to move through." Sometimes, I would say, "You know you're right." We could have an honest dialogue about where I was stuck, and we both processed and learned more about different facets of the experience.

We need all sorts of friends in our lives: people we have fun with, serve with, work with, and those we might only see occasionally.

We were created for community. Whether we are extroverts, introverts, or ambiverts, each of us experiences a stirring for connection. Everyone wants to be known, loved, and in community on some level and in some way.

Stormy friends: No, I don't mean the disruptive kind. Keep close an inner circle of those who really know you when you travel through a difficult storm. When I was in my active infertility season, three people linked arms with me during that journey. One friend had been through infertility and was on the other side, one was walking through it at the same time, and one had never been through infertility. Each one offered a different perspective and proved influential during that life tsunami. A variety of friends can occupy these positions and walk well with us.

Mentor friends: These make up a different circle of friends who bring a richness to our journey. I've had several speaking into my life, some for many years and some for a shorter period of time. What I love about these relationships is that they seemed to authentically unfold and blossom. Pay attention to people further ahead of you in life. Maybe you know someone in the same industry, church, or neighborhood who can offer wisdom and guidance when needed. These friends give my life a depth that I could never find anywhere else, and I appreciate them more than words can say. Along with seeking mentors ahead of you, be on the lookout for someone coming along behind you to speak into their life and encourage them along the way. Both sides of this mentorship bring a beautiful intergenerational layer to our life.

God: For me, the foundation of faith anchors everything in life. When the waves come crashing and the rain lashes, I find peace that escapes any normal understanding. When life looks calm, I have the same peace that all is well and life abounds here and evermore.

Myself: Yes, I am in community with myself. You are in community with yourself. How do we treat ourselves? Do we offer positive, healthy self-talk? Get plenty of rest and good nutrition? Seek healthy boundaries and improvement when needed?

Do we invite a therapist or counselor in who has our best interests at heart? Will someone listen and offer a different perspective or help nudge us to revise life action or offer a healthy framework to follow during times of distress? Depending on their knowledge and how they inspire coping or change, they can help us view things from a different angle, shape new options, and maintain life flexibility needed when strong winds blow through.

We all need someone who says, "I believe in you." Some days, we might need to be the one to say it to ourselves. Seriously. Look in the mirror, stare into your own eyes and say, "I believe in you." I had to do this the other day and add, "God has amazing plans for you. Do the next thing." Sometimes in lonely moments, we need a healthy dose of self-care and talk.

Reach Out to Others

We will often walk through lonely times in life. After we acknowledge it, let's make an effort to reach out to those in need who might struggle through similar circumstances. What tools can you offer?

Sometimes just a listening ear provides something they need and will help you feel a sense of purpose. Allow others into your struggle to do the same for you (and for them!).

One of the most basic things we can do is reach in with an offer of food. We all need food and water to keep going, and when life tasks feel overwhelming, we can overlook this basic need for sustenance.

After the tornado hit, gas and electricity were off for days. Most side streets stayed roadblocked to traffic, with access limited to residents and specific city service teams. Houses had no available refrigeration, working microwaves, or stoves.

One food outreach came via a local church that loved their neighbors well. For several days, they drove a golf cart up and down one of the main streets in between traumatized neighborhoods. The back of the golf cart held a huge ice chest with individually packaged sandwiches, bags of chips, and bottled water they handed out to the police officers, homeowners, city employees, clean-up crews, anyone in the neighborhood who wanted food and drink.

Within a couple of days, a local grocery store set up two eighteen-wheeler food trailers, tables, and chairs in a parking lot a few blocks away. They offered freshly cooked food to anyone who showed up, all day for many days. What a beautiful sight to see people gathering for a meal or carrying food to others, all in the name of "together recovery."

Show Up

Show up! Sometimes storm debris and its aftermath (or the "in-between") causes sensory overload and jumbled thinking for the survivor. Don't ask someone experiencing life turbulence what you can do to help—this puts the burden and stress on them.

Spend a little time thinking generally about basics you could or would offer to someone in need and, as situations arise, tweak the details for specific people and circumstances. What you offer will need to be appropriate for how well you know someone, the time you can allow, the cost, and their specific situation.

In the extremely raw emotional time after the breakup of my marriage, my lifelong friend, Kelly, and her husband, Joe, took me on several dinner dates. At the time, I kept mostly to myself, feeling heaps of negative emotions and great isolation. Once Kelly learned the reality of my situation, she called one day and said, "Joe and I are going to dinner tomorrow night and want to take you on a dinner date." The way she phrased it, coupled with the trust I have for them both, led to my surprising *yes* answer.

When they arrived to pick me up, both came to the door to get me—something about the gesture touched my heart in a deep way. Over dinner, they offered their calming presence, listening ears, great empathy, and lots of fun memories of our friendship. At the end of the night, they drove me home and both got out to walk me safely to my front door. I've been on several dinner dates with them and found them to be such friendship-deepening, joyful, supportive, let's-do-life-together, soul-feeding times. I'm grateful beyond measure.

If you are part of a couple and have a friend recently divorced or widowed, a dinner date can offer such support, thoughtfulness, and care. Just sitting at a table and offering companionship will mean the world to your friend who has suffered lots of layers of loss.

Post-tornado, several friends and community members wanted to do something to assist. Within the outpouring of care, I discovered the challenges involved with helping others know how to help. It was overwhelming to figure out what to tell them I needed when I didn't even know myself.

Also, in an effort for law enforcement to prevent looting and scamming the first couple of weeks, each time we walked into the affected neighborhood, we had to show ID to prove we lived there. Somehow, my friend Suzanne got through, rang the doorbell, and said, "I'm here—show me what you need next." I seriously didn't even know. I walked her around the house, showing the damage, and we got to the bedroom with broken glass and leaves still strewn everywhere. At this point, we didn't even have electricity back on, so the vacuum wouldn't work. She said, "Go do what you need to do; I'm going to clean up in here."

A little while later, I came back in to see her picking up large pieces of glass (she brought her own contractor trash bags), shaking the bedcover over the carpet, and then sweeping the carpet to get up as much debris as possible without a working vacuum cleaner (she went exploring and found the broom on her own). Not all of the small pieces came up, but enough was done to bring a bit of order back to the room and make it not feel so alarming anymore.

It took a minute for me to just accept that she came to work, but she did—and she meant it. I had to let go of my "thanks, I can do it myself" and let her help me. She blessed me by showing up, noticing what needed to be done and could be accomplished. I gave her a sense of satisfaction in being able to do something tangible to help her friend.

I allowed her to reach in.

As we think about ways we can help our close circle of people, we can also find meaningful ways to reach out to our communities.

The Essential Elements of Community

Self-Care

There is a reason flight attendants instruct passengers traveling with children to put their oxygen mask on first, then put the child's mask in place.

Long ago, when I heard this, I thought it sounded strange. I mean, shouldn't the adults help kids first?

Children need us to take care of ourselves so we can help them. If we pass out from lack of oxygen, we can't help them.

The same principle applies to ourselves and our community.

I want to remind you, again, that you are part of your community! What does your inner voice say to you? I confess I've endured lots of negative self-talk, and often this inner dialogue validates either my made-up insecurity or negative words from someone whose opinion and validation I sought. "See, even they don't believe you can do this. Why bother?"

If you can relate, I have a question for you:

Would you allow someone to speak to a loved one the way you speak to yourself?

Let's treat ourselves with the kindness and respect we so readily seek to offer strangers, family, and friends. Put your oxygen mask on first—take care of yourself (including self-talk). If we can't demonstrate care and grace to ourselves, how successful and genuine will we be with others?

Other-Care

We can also practice this healthy talk with people who really know us or "get" us. Let's be open with others we trust and then listen when they speak into our lives. Let's believe them when they tell us they believe in us! Let's freely offer them that same positivity and encouragement.

Unity

Take a step of "tens" toward healthier interactions and more unity.

When someone says something rude, count slowly to ten. Breathe and relax; stay calm, reserve any response, whether in person or online.

Wait.

If online, we might wait even longer; it could be beneficial to wait overnight to see if we even still feel a need to comment the next day. So often, an immediate response to someone's words toward us only serves to increase the animosity.

Ten counts.

An interval of ten slow counts to calmly respond or even quietly excuse ourselves, if necessary.

Take a breather and reflect: What events or small acts of kindness have you seen that promote unity in community?

We *must* invest in one another's lives, speaking encouragement and hope. There are many who have no one doing this for them. Let's be intentional with care through our words. Jesus said loving God and loving one another are the greatest commandments. We need him, and we need his tangible love through each other as we travel through life.

A Closer Look: The Winds of Disability

When Mike was twenty years old, he took a motorcycle "trip of a lifetime" with several high school friends. On that trip, a car hit him and he suffered a broken back and a severed spinal cord. As a result, for the majority of his adult life, he has lived as a paraplegic and wheelchair user.

In hindsight, he shared that the accident reinforced the importance of God, his family, friends, and community in life. People showed up, not only for him but also for his parents and brothers. He spent two-and-a-half months in rehab located sixty miles from his home, and not a day went by that he didn't have someone visit. "People showed how much they loved me. They didn't know what to do, but they were there when I needed someone to talk to."[32]

Mike walked through a dark time in life as he considered what the future might hold for him in his new physical reality. He had many willing to walk with him and help him know he wasn't by himself.

So often in life, we all get caught up in daily busyness and tasks. Let's make sure we pay attention to who in our sphere needs our presence for a brief time or for the duration of a new existence. As we are able, let's give them our time and attention and allow others to do the same for us when we need it. We all need to know we're in this life together!

Prior to his accident, Mike loved running. After his accident and through a long journey, he met others with physical disabilities and got involved in wheelchair/adaptive sports.

The opportunity to return to sports gave him a new lift and purpose. In 1985, he even pushed his wheelchair from Fairbanks, Alaska, to Washington, DC. God brought along his best friend from high school to handle the details of the trip and get the word out (there was no social media at the time) to TV stations and police in each town along the way. He used the trip to raise money for the rehab center that took care of him. His wife, Sharyn, shared, "Mike wanted to show others there is still a lot of life you can fully live with a disability."[33]

In the early 2000s, Mike went to work for Joni and Friends, an international ministry serving people living with a disability. This is how he met his wife, Sharyn. They have been married for twelve years and co-founded a Christian organization called Powered to Move, where they build community while offering opportunities for healthy activity and experiences.

Their motto is "Move What You Can." Mike describes their community as people with disabilities, able-bodied athletes, and non-athletes, all coming together to spend time and share life.

"Just because I'm disabled doesn't mean I only have disabled friends. Technology brought in the ability for disabled persons to get out and enjoy different activities, social atmosphere, sharing life with other people, which is what the Christian life is all about."[34]

Chapter Fourteen

Threads of Friendship

*H*ot summer days remind me of joyful times in childhood with the neighborhood kids. Playing tag, running around, climbing trees, riding bicycles.

Especially riding bikes.

Sneakers pedaling as fast as small feet allow, wind blowing through our hair, singing silly songs as we ride down alleys and streets, exploring the space where we live.

Freedom.

Friendship.

Fun.

I especially reflect on those carefree days when I hear current news of people from that youthful world.

My brother's best friend died a few years ago. They are older than I am, but I've heard about their lifetime of friendship for as long as I can remember.

When I spoke with my brother the day after his friend's passing, he told me about many of their school friends who texted, called, showed up, and offered prayer. In the midst of tremendous sadness, they came together. As my brother beautifully put it, "We began life together. Now we're ending it together."

Such a loving yet debilitating sentiment.

Oh, that we all had lifelong friends like this group.

Not too long after, I read a social media post from one of my high school friends reporting on a near tragedy. She was a passenger in a single-engine plane that day and experienced complete engine failure at 8,000 feet. Thankfully, they were able to land safely.

No injuries; everyone was okay. What a relief.

I share these stories not to bring you down but to encourage you to positive action.

As I think about cherished memories of long-ago friends, I consider how we individually and together can affect positive change in the world.

I reflect on the fun we all had riding bikes together as kids. We are each unique individuals and have encountered different life journeys, but we share foundational memories and experiences.

The wheel of a bicycle is such a beautiful example of our lives. The spokes connect in two places. They start at a unifying point or hub, then spread outward to connect to the rim of the wheel to help move the bike forward.

Can't we each be the hub of a wheel in our areas of influence? Whether by faith in God or a common desire to simply live by the Golden Rule, we could each spread love and respect to affect change in our corner of the world.

What if we seek to speak only kind words, type positive comments, or stop ourselves before we respond to negativity?

What if we capture harsh thoughts and mentally shut the door on them or reframe them in a positive way so our thought patterns change, which will then affect our behaviors as well?

I refuse to give up hope on our common respect and dignity for one another. We played together as children, grew up alongside one another. Let's move into tomorrow committed to being the hopeful, positive, encouraging hub of our life wheel.

We. Can. Do. This.

A Closer Look: The Winds of Life Storms

My friend Taurus and I share similar experiences. We also have vastly different backgrounds and shaping circumstances.

I consider our friendship a great blessing and hold sacred our ability to come together, join in healthy conversation, and open one another's eyes to different layers of our life stories. We met in grad school. I'm white; she's black. I grew up on one side of our city; she grew up on the other. I'm childless; she's a mom. I'm a hugger; she's not (she'll laugh when she reads this sentence!).

We both love Jesus and seek to truly know what motivates people to a particular action or reaction beyond the surface layer of existence. We love to laugh, and we both seek to live out a life of creativity and care.

Our conversation on the podcast came at a critical time in our country and the world at large. Between the pandemic and racial issues, economic challenges, and the heat of political races, life felt overwhelming and chaotic. In a quest to better understand, clarify, and make sense of a variety of situations, I knew I needed to have an honest conversation with her about the cultural and societal storm clouds and fallout.

Before that, we talked about the literal tornado that blew through a large part of our city. As she shared her tornado experiences (yes, plural!), we compared literal, natural disaster storms to the fabric of society storms looming over us all.

Taurus shared her experience of a direct hit by a tornado. "The storm can be extremely ugly, but the clean-up process is crucial."[35] The physical, post-storm recovery overwhelms all senses. As with the aftermath of tornado force winds, the first step begins with an assessment of what debris we can remove and clear a path for incoming help.

I remember walking down the street the morning after the tornado—I didn't even recognize where I was. So many fallen trees in yards and streets, some roofs ripped off, bricks tossed like a child's upturned toy box, pink insulation scattered in every direction. Neighbors first worked to clear the streets by cutting and moving trees and branches to the side and stacking broken bricks and shingles on the curbs.

Taurus pointed out that after a storm, even though people live in the neighborhood and have different tools and capabilities, we still need the community at large to come and help in ways we can't help ourselves—tree experts with chain saws, bulldozers, city utilities, gas companies, electricians, and clean-up crews with appropriate equipment.

During our look at this process, we recognized a similar thread when we experience a devastating virus that takes the world and communities by storm. Something previously unknown, a silent, invisible threat, created a sense of cloistering.

We can sit in the middle of the fallout and just keep scrolling, viewing, and listening to the same voices offering similar information, or we can seek a healthy balance of information and opinions.

When a natural disaster hits, people gather to hug, cry, and console one another. Outsiders grab tools and rush in to help where needed. No one asks "qualifying" questions to ensure that people deserve help. Our instinct inspires us to gain an understanding, take what we can provide, and move toward others in the mystifying debris. Taurus explained:

> "When a tornado hits, you're all out together and despondent; you cry and hold each other and say, 'oh my gosh, we have nothing, but we're still here.' You see it on television all the time. I think the danger is when it festers. So, if you look at the current times, filled with racial unrest, there is a tendency to isolate simply because it's an uncomfortable conversation. It's easier to talk about me losing everything in a tornado; it's not easy for me to talk about the history of this country and what it has done to us as a culture."[36]

Wow! She called that out so clearly. We've allowed our differences, miscommunication, injustice, history, and fear to create another layer of storm. In order to move forward, truly love one another, and restore a sense of unity, we all must take the first steps of a renewed willingness to offer grace and listening ears. Much awaits to be done.

As with any physical storm, we need to assess where we stand and begin to move our preconceived ideas to the side so we can have healthy conversations and take those first steps of rebuilding. I know it won't be easy, and I know that we didn't cover all the things that need to be in place, but willingness and openness to listen and learn one another's story will help lay the vibrant foundation of hopeful community together.

As Taurus offered, "You want to know what a solution is? Build a relationship with somebody who doesn't look like you. It's very simple."[37]

Let's go out and build.

Who Makes Up Your Community?

Spend time reviewing your connecting points and determining who makes up your community of people.

Church, work, neighbors, life friends, school, your children and their activities, volunteer opportunities? Take a few minutes to think about your outer circles and write them down here or in a *Winds of Change* journal or companion guide.

_____

_____

_____

_____

_____

Different seasons in life train us up with more empathy and practical compassion. As we move forward, we can reach out and help others through their own lonely days.

We can also be intentional and invite trusted friends into our experiences.

Don't do the dark of night alone, figuratively and literally.

In the middle of the night darkness, have a battery-operated candle in a votive on your night table. When the mental and emotional clouds mushroom in the quiet darkness and you feel the overwhelm of anxiety growing by leaps and bounds, sit up and flip the switch on the battery candle to shine a small light and disrupt the dark.

During dark moments, I read aloud a favorite Bible verse handwritten on a card. Then I lay down and look at the tiny light of the "candle" and remind myself I am not alone. I have God, and I have people who care.

Keep a pen and notebook to write down thoughts that inspire you. Handwriting gives you a tangible way to combat the fear and anxiety. (Don't type the note in your phone; that will tempt you to start scrolling, which can start a path of middle-of-the-night comparison and more worry.)

Write a favorite Scripture or inspirational, comforting quote on a card and keep it next to the votive to read when you need that brief overnight reassurance.

As we evaluate our meaningful community, let's be intentional about inviting trusted friends and family into our journey—those who have our best interests at heart. Isolation can become a lonely, unhealthy place when activated for too long. In our pain, let's take a really brave, deep breath and invite somebody in to just be with us.

Remember as well, when someone invites us in, maintain a willing heart to show up for them, offer our presence, and not try to fix them or their challenges. Just listen and be with them.

Let's reach out to each other.

Don't suffer in silence.

Social Media: Creating Healthy Community

We've talked about the negativity we can face while publicly engaging with others. Let's look at how we can use social media platforms in supportive, positive ways.

I have personally witnessed outreach to the tornado victims in my area and have seen people come together in neighborhoods struck by natural disasters throughout the country and the world.

The tragedy of family illness and the heartbreak of death rally communities to come together through social platforms to help and support each other. People post stories and articles asking for volunteers and donations for those in challenging situations. Organizations send out notifications of available resources for people in need. Individuals communicate the offer of assistance and tools to help with unfolding events that require immediate action. Social media has given us the ability to reach out to our communities in positive ways.

When we put aside our differences and display our compassionate humanity, we are using important resources in the best way possible.

Chapter Fifteen

Life Together

*I*n the movie *Harry Potter and the Order of the Phoenix*,[38] Harry and Luna Lovegood have a conversation about feeling alone. Luna explains that she and her father believe Harry—that He Who Must Not Be Named is back. Harry says, "Thanks, seems you're about the only ones that do." Luna replies, "I don't think that's true. But I suppose that's how he wants you to feel."

Harry asks, "What d'you mean?" Luna then offers great wisdom, "Well, if I were You Know Who, I'd want you to feel cut off from everyone else, 'cause if it's just you alone, you're not as much of a threat."

Please take great care with your isolation and stay connected with your community. They can provide depth and meaning in a variety of ways.

My great-nephew, who is nonverbal, grew up in a nurturing community and school system. His high school graduation exemplified in one evening how much the larger community can positively affect one family and engage a ripple effect that reaches others.

A Graduation Moment

As each graduate's name came over the loudspeaker, they strode quickly across the stage to collect their diplomas. The end of the alphabet finally arrived, and I heard my great-nephew's name called.

Then came the moment that took my breath away.

He took a few faltering steps.

A wave of fellow graduating seniors jumped to their feet, clapping loudly. Within seconds the entire large senior class stood clapping, whistling, and yelling for him. Teachers in chairs onstage joined the impromptu celebration, and the other teachers in the audience chimed in too.

The thundering roar of loud whistles and cheering rose to the heights of the historic hall as my great-nephew (with his teacher close behind) made the journey to his principal and diploma.

The long evening of rapid recitation of graduate names came to a one-minute standstill as they paused to give this young man his full time in the spotlight. His uneven yet joy-filled gait took him the length of the stage—pausing occasionally to look out over the cheering sea of his peers and teachers.

As I stood with our family, surrounded by such a joyful noise, I could barely see what I was recording on my phone due to the welling tears in my eyes.

Honestly?

I wanted to fall to the floor and weep with overwhelming gratefulness at the outpouring of love for him. The wave of enthusiastic support and care curled around not only him but also his family.

This moment-in-time recognition of a twenty-two-year journey celebrated a beautiful, nontypical life: difficult steps that for others were an ability taken for granted, life basics achieved over many years, and the joy and love he brought to each of their lives.

He met his unique requirements to receive his graduation diploma from an extraordinary high school in a school system that embraced and assisted him from day one.

I have watched from afar (we live about 1,500 miles apart) as he grew. His parents, brother, extended family, neighbors, school system, therapists, and teachers surrounded him with great love and support along the way.

Employers and co-workers offered grace, care, and understanding to his parents for unexpected absences and unplanned medical events that occurred on a fairly regular basis.

True community stood encapsulated in one minute on a high school graduation stage.

What a privilege to witness.

Helping kids and adults with intellectual disabilities grow to their fullest potential takes grit, perseverance, and lots of hard work. The reward of knowing them makes it well worth any output necessary to meet their needs. These unique individuals offer back what the rest of us often miss in our busyness, stress, and distraction—the simple joy of a heartfelt smile and daily life milestones.

May I offer my thanks to any of you involved with persons who have intellectual disabilities?

We are one big community and must spur one another on in love!

If you know someone who has a family member with intellectual disabilities, will you send them a text or note of encouragement this week? Taking a moment to honor their life will mean the world to them and their family.

A Closer Look: The Winds of Special Needs

Kristen's love for her intellectually disabled son, Jason,[39] shines through in her commitment to him and her family. My niece's daily attitude (choosing joy and living a full life every single day) offers encouragement to those around her.

Kristen and her husband, Gary, had no idea about Jason's special needs until they began to notice that he missed several infant milestones. The pediatrician said their older son had been ahead of the game and to give it some time. Jason didn't improve, and then he had a strange allergic reaction. This led them to see a neurologist and begin some physical therapy.

"I thought at the time, okay, we'll do this for a month, and we'll be right on track—and never knew it was going to be the life we would live."[40] For the first five years of his life, they tried to figure out his diagnosis. Meanwhile, Jason wasn't walking, he wasn't eating well, he had fine motor and gross motor delays, and he wasn't speaking. But he was an alert, joyful (with typical mood exceptions), happy individual.

"I'm thankful I have someone who can look me in the eye and I know what he's thinking or feeling, or if he is happy or not, even though he doesn't always have the words."[41]

Although it took years to get some kind of diagnosis, their family experienced beautiful support from family, friends, their public school system, and community. There were bumps along the way with different people, and Kristen expressed gratefulness for those willing to show up, offer inclusion for Jason, ask questions about how to practically help, and give her a listening ear.

Friends would call from the local coffee place and say, "I'm in line and want to bring you something. Tell me what to order and I'll bring it by." One friend asked Kristen to send her a very specific grocery list including pictures because she was headed to the grocery store the next day and wanted to take care of that task for her. Jason has always had life-threatening food allergies, and labels have to be carefully examined for hidden ingredients. There are foods and added substances that could literally kill him if he eats them. She isn't being overprotective or particular. "Since he is non-verbal, he can't say 'that made my throat a little itchy' or 'my stomach hurts after eating that.' We don't have that feedback."[42]

We can offer practical assistance to our friends in thoughtful little ways. Too often, the recipient of our help feels like a burden or is too mentally exhausted to try to explain what they need. Once they know their friend is headed to the cleaners, they don't feel bad about getting a bag of clothes together to be dropped off too.

What can we do to help those we don't know and may encounter in public? Often, when we see someone who is physically or intellectually disabled or different, we tend to look the other way, walk on by, or maybe we're just too busy to notice. A couple of years ago, Kristen and I took Jason on a trip to Walt Disney World. She wanted him to experience a "typical" kid's vacation. What an amazing trip!

Every cast member, character, medical person, chef, really anyone we encountered, offered loving, caring, accommodating, magical engagement to him and to us. My niece shipped supplies ahead of time, made sure we had an accessible room to meet his needs, and created an open dialogue for every meal prepared for him. One of the most beautiful elements of the cast? Not one of them was afraid to say hello. The ones who saw his "my first visit" button with his name written on it took the time to look him in the eye and greet him by name. We could tell he felt so included, and he spread his overwhelming joy to them as well.

As we stood in line for one ride, a little girl began to talk to Jason, ignoring his wheelchair and his inability to give words in response. She excitedly peppered him with thoughts and questions.

"Well, I like this . . ."

"Are you having fun?"

"I'm five; how old are you?"

She just kept up a steady stream of one-sided conversation while we all waited to move forward toward the ride.

When her mom realized she was talking to people behind them and noticed Jason in his adult wheelchair, she quickly asked Kristen if her daughter was bothering us or him with her questions.

Kristen told her how wonderful it was that her daughter treated him like anyone else.

When we reached the platform, the little girl and her parents boarded the ride and she turned back to tell Jason to have a good time. Kristen and I were floored by the normalcy she extended to him. We also felt gratitude for her parents, who didn't turn her around in embarrassment because they didn't know what to say. Instead, they allowed her to have freedom with questions that my niece age-appropriately answered about Jason's inability to talk and his need for a wheelchair. As Kristen remembered that experience, she explained the importance of the child's conversation.

> "To have someone so innocent at that age do something so normal was huge, and I think for both of us it was like, wow! People aren't afraid of us. There were plenty of other people who would say hello, but she

just didn't care. She just wanted to talk to us about what she liked the most and hey, I like your stroller, is red your favorite color? She was so sweet. I just wish more people were like that. So often, kids will ask innocently, 'What's wrong with him? Why is he in that chair?' The parents don't want to offend, so they say, 'Shhhhh or We'll talk about it later.' It's perfectly fine to say, 'Let's go ask him.' It might take a little more time, but it's a whole different attitude, and it will teach people that it's okay to talk about what's going on and offer the opportunity to give an answer with honesty versus giving a negative experience."[43]

Ultimately, it is all about human connection. We can show love and care to other parents, families, and children by sharing their burden and experiencing their joy.

Sharing joy and encouragement comes in all forms. Look for opportunities to support others, even in seemingly little ways. I guarantee your words and actions can have an impact for good in someone else's life.

Voices of Encouragement

During a retreat weekend, I decided to try a new activity: crate stacking. It was a bigger challenge than I expected, and it reminded me how important it is for us to use our voices to encourage each other.

With hands outstretched, I held my breath to balance and focus on catching each cube of plastic tossed up to me. Once caught, I bent down to place it carefully and securely so I could then step up onto it.

With each crate I stacked, I gained a little more height in the air . . . the higher I went, the less stable I felt. In fact, I couldn't believe the difficulty in balancing on the plastic surface, catching the next crate, bending down to put it securely in place, and then taking the next step up to continue the climb . . . all while wearing a harness, helmet, and two safety wires attached to the tall pole behind.

What looked super easy from the ground translated into a very different story once I gained a true crate view. The climb challenged me and stirred a competitive impulse to stack and conquer a certain number of crates. I couldn't have done any of it without the camp counselor tossing the crates up in the air to me and calling out instructions. Or without the new friends shouting out encouragement and helpful tips from below.

I didn't make it as high up as I wanted, and the fun activity proved a much bigger obstacle than it looked from below, but it promoted teamwork, encouragement, and a big dose of "I can do this!"

When we face challenges and feel all alone in our pain, the people around us live out a vital role in our lives when they offer support. When we all learn a little more about different life situations and ways to help, it prepares our hearts and hands for practical compassion to reach out with care and empathy to those in need.

We all need friends, loved ones, and even strangers cheering us on when we face an unknown climb.

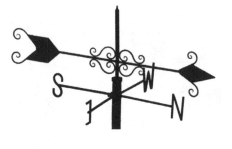

Part Three

Dreams

Chapter Sixteen

Moving Through Grief

*W*hat do we do with unrealized dreams? Those events in life that never come to fruition or the ones that take our breath away with the brutality of loss?

Some we might expect, but many surprise us in unexpected ways. When negative winds blow, the events and emotions that follow result in gales of grief, regret, and sadness. There might be an expectation of a death, but the reality of that loss peels another layer of difficult day-to-day coping.

- The unrealized dream of becoming a mom or dad brings different waves and pangs of loss. These can occur throughout the process of realizing that certain ages and stages won't be reached in the way we once hoped.
- The death of a spouse at any age is painful. When this occurs in earlier adulthood, the grief journey of the surviving spouse includes additional loss layers during future family celebrations and milestones.

- Parents whose young adult children have died face lifelong grief and questions about what "might have been."
- Grown children with the realities of aging parents or spouses whose partners suffer from dementia. The daily loss of a once healthy person forgetting who they are and losing the ability to recognize people or even understand basic objects or tasks presents devastating heartbreak for loved ones.

If you know someone in the trauma of an unrealized dream, will you stand ready to come alongside them with whatever you can offer—your presence, listening ear, or errand assistance? Check in with them and check on them, especially the ones who *seem* to stand strong and tall in the midst of the gale-force winds. They might look like they have a handle on the situation and their coping skills; however, their brave front might hide a desperate loneliness and isolation.

If you find yourself keeping it all together and facing the brutal blows of winds whipping around you, will you please reach out to others and let them know you need their presence and a shoulder to lean on?

We all need to know we don't walk alone.

In the midst of our expectations and different outcomes, so often, we don't know if life winds will blow us off course or on course. We find our bearing and dream anyway.

Grief comes in many forms. When a thread of grief weaves through our life, we need to realize, name, and address it along the way. The waves come at different times, and everyone's journey looks unique. Just know that grief is real and requires our attention to address it in healthy and appropriate ways, not only for ourselves but also for our friends and loved ones.

Navigating Grief

Grief can creep up on us, and any unexpected trauma can trigger deep feelings within. When we watch our friends face this experience, we struggle to know what help we can provide and how to support them. But the following suggestions have proven useful:

1. Offer practical help. Your sacrificial support provides more care than you may know. If you can give the commitment, let your friend know your availability to help at a moment's notice. (They might not accept your help for a while. That is okay. Be flexible, offer grace, and assure them you are there for them. This is about what *they* want and need.)

2. Don't put the burden on them. Express the help you plan to provide. Offer to bring dinner, watch the kids, take care of their laundry. When you ask them what help they need, it creates an added burden to make another decision.

   Simply offer your willing availability. Many times, the best support you can give is to be present. You don't even have to say a thing! Show up with something you can do while just sitting with them: Bring a book to read, or that knitting project, or bring a puzzle to quietly work on together.

3. When your family member or friend experiences the loss of someone, don't fear saying their name. When people pass away, loved ones want to hear their name and share stories as a way to value and honor them and to learn about special memories from others. Each conversation can bring a little more peace, comfort, and healing.

A Closer Look: The Winds of Grief

My friend René experienced a traumatic loss in her life over twenty years ago. She joined me on the podcast to share her story and offer her perspective on how to help someone in a grief situation.[44]

As she explained, the month of May has the potential to bring a large wave of emotional pain. May days include Mother's Day, her only child's birth date, and his death date. Even with a long journey working through her grief, May can still bring waves of overwhelming pain and remembrance. Her son, Christopher, lived three thousand miles away when he was killed. In the immediate aftermath of her grief storm, the distance added a layer of guilt weight because she wasn't close by when he died.

She described how she felt after initially learning the news about her son. The numbness, dismissiveness (*oh, this couldn't have happened*), and the grief fog proved overwhelming for a long, long time. As we talked, I described how I felt at that time, being a close friend of hers who lived many miles away, hearing the pain, disbelief, and detachment in her voice every time I called to check on her.

René wisely shared, "Everybody has their journey in their own way and their own time. You don't get over it—you get *through* it. The best thing you did for me was listen, and maybe it was just to listen to me cry."[45]

This might be the first time I really understood that we don't have to walk through the same storm in life to learn something from it. When we hear how others coped with their pain, or gained courage, or what someone did to help them—whatever the situation—we can adapt many principle ideas to use in our own life stories that will help not only ourselves but also our friends and families.

Everyone has their own journey and experiences. Feeling like we don't walk alone provides a large measure of comfort. At the time of René's raw grief, I accidentally helped her feel more assured by continuing to reach out, check on her, and listen. I really didn't know what to do at the time; I just knew my friend sat in an unimaginable pit of grief and I was miles away and needed to do *something* to help her know I cared. "We don't want to feel alone in our pain. Getting out of the pain, fog, and malaise, and the desire to start living again, helps us start reaching."[46]

Of the many helpful steps we discussed, three stand out:

1. Every person's grief looks and feels different and has no definitive timeline. Grief is not linear. Offering support, grace, and understanding as friends, loved ones, and community members walk through grief helps them feel a sort of grounding in their steps. There are certainly times to encourage them to reengage in their life but only when there exists a proven track record of love and trust.

2. Show our willingness to consistently show up. When we give our presence, time, and listening hearts, we build trust by continuing to return and not walk away. Our friends in pain notice this persistence of care and will begin to open up, bit by bit. We reach in and coax them to reach out and walk together to rebuild a different, solid path that helps them move through the storm of grief.

3. Never, ever tell them to get over it or remind them of how much time has passed since the event. Trust me, they know the exact amount of time, whether it occurred a

week ago or twenty years ago. Grief has no time limit or expiration date.

Whenever you experience grief, be gentle with yourself and give yourself time and space. Just sit in it when you need to and reach out when needed.

If you walk with someone in the middle of overwhelming grief, let them know you're there for them with physical presence, texts, and voice messages. In the midst of these messages, let them know there is no pressure to respond to each one. Give them the freedom to accept them and know that you are communicating your care. Often the need to respond to everyone's messages might feel daunting. Assure them you do not expect them to reach back every time but that you want them to know you are thinking of and praying for them.

Don't try to fix their situation with actions or words. You can't.

A New View of Grief

Grief can be paralyzing when we can't imagine our future without the person who is gone or when we have to say goodbye to a life dream. The realness of everyday absence triggers raw pain, and the projection of that reality onto future life events adds an additional layer of mourning during new seasons.

My father died many years ago, and, due to circumstances beyond anyone's control, his memorial service took place on my birthday.

At the time, I remember a brief feeling of horror that, for the rest of my life, I would share my birthday with the anniversary of the great loss of my dad. The unbearable year of "firsts" after he died, all I could do was dread that anniversary/birthday week. I knew we couldn't avoid the original situation that required his service's scheduling, and I tried really hard to put on my adulting self and just get through it. I didn't even want to celebrate the next few birthdays and couldn't imagine a time when I would look forward to one again.

Over time, I began to think of this annual event as an honor to share with my dad. Now, I'm much further down the road and my birthday feels like a loving tribute to his life, my life, and my daughter/father relationship with him. I think of it as a day that I am privileged to share, that I *get* to share, with him.

Understand that it took a long time to get to this emotional and mental place. I trudged through a mountain of struggling steps toward this goal, but each one was worth it.

Not long ago, I heard a beautiful, emotional summary from someone else who lost their father, and I really want to embrace this direction of emotion and thought for any future loss in life. The show was about the life (and death) of actor John Ritter. Full of show clips, life stories, interviews with friends and fellow actors, the celebration resounded with his impact on family, friends, co-workers, and fans.

During the show, his son, Jason Ritter, shared a poignant thought that forever changed how I will try to approach grief after losing someone. "One of the things that I try to do is look at his life. Instead of feeling like I was reading this beautiful book and all of a sudden the last ten chapters were ripped out, I started to look at it as that was the whole book. That's the whole story, and there was so much beauty in his life."[47]

Ritter's description offers a way to reframe loss and helps ease the raw emotion and thoughts of an unknown future without a loved one. It doesn't erase the pain we feel when we miss someone we dearly love, but it can change our perspective and lead us in a healthy direction toward healing.

Chapter Seventeen

Taking Time to Dream

"*I*'m telling you . . . Broadway, here I come!"

"What?"

"If I could do anything in the world, you want to know what I would do? I would be Jennifer Holliday, singing my way through the musical *Dreamgirls*."

When people gather around my table for a meal, I like to ask get-to-know-you questions. A favorite is the "What would you do?" query. In other words, "If talent, skills, money, education, experience, and opportunity were not factors or roadblocks, what would you do? If you could do *anything*, what would it be?"

I would be Jennifer Holliday for one night on Broadway.

The question also brings new insight for friends who know each other well, resulting in much laughter and a deeper understanding of one another. It is a fun way to know someone on a different level and offers surprising discoveries about people and their dreams.

Dreams Do Come True

Debbie Cunningham and I met for coffee to talk about her pursuit of lifelong dreams later in life.

After an early career in music and then time dedicated to raising her children, she had a moment of realization one day as she swept her kitchen floor. A song came on and she thought, "That's what I want to do." She knew she wanted to be a jazz singer.

She prayed about getting into that specific market, and at the age of forty, Debbie became a jazz artist. With the encouragement and support of her husband, she pursued her studies, recorded her first album at forty-one, and has been going strong ever since. The song "Fly," available on her website, offers us encouragement to dream and try.[48]

Not only is Debbie a successful jazz musician, but she also recently published a book about marriage.[49] She described her writing dream by sharing, "I never planned to write a book about marriage, but the encouragement of my fans and mentors inspired me to take the leap."[50]

As we discussed earlier, our community can be a source of support and wonderful ideas when we engage them in our lives and dreams!

▼▼▼

A Closer Look: The Winds of a Dream

Once I visited a stunning vista on the way up to a harrowing mountain pass. I remember stopping and soaking in the majesty of the view. When I reflect on big life dreams, that mental picture shows up. The awesome, overwhelming size and beauty of God's creation where we can gain perspective, release stress, grab inner peace, and take time and space to let our minds wander and creatively dream.

What do we do when we have a mountain-sized dream and we keep saying no or think we aren't capable of achieving it? (Sometimes, even smaller dreams feel insurmountable too!) So often, we deny our dream. Then, if we pay attention, we might see God putting people in our path or events taking place that give us a small nugget of affirmation to go for it.

How can we transform our fear or uncertainty about even the possibility of conquering a mountain of a dream? My pastor and friend, Neil Tomba, did just that in fulfilling his eighteen-year dream of a bike ride across the United States. It began as an idea he had in the mountains of Colorado. Then he saw how, over time, God brought people and events together to keep pointing him to this *yes* and to eventually live out the reality. "You can't forever say no because one day you're not going to have a choice to ever say yes."[51]

In June 2019, he pedaled his bicycle from Santa Monica, California, to Annapolis, Maryland. He pedaled three thousand miles in thirty-three days, accompanied by his co-riders and two vehicles carrying the rest of the team.

His goal? To travel the country and stop to engage in meaningful conversations about faith and life with total strangers he met along the way. He wrote a book,[52] and production of a movie journaling his ride is currently in the works.

Who doesn't love a story about someone dreaming big and rising to the challenge? In reality, taking the bold step to try a dream requires a big bunch of courage. What can we do? As Neil wisely advised, the first thing we must do is say yes. As we move forward, we can continue to affirm the direction or maybe we can stop and reconsider.

What can we do to take practical steps in the process of affirmation or even when reconsidering or reshaping the dream?

- Pray about how we are wired and things we feel passionate about in life.

- Pay attention to the people God puts in our path and information we encounter that leads in an affirming direction toward accomplishing the dream.
- Gather supportive people around us. We all need friends who offer truth in love. Some may jump in to cheerlead what we pursue and bring others along, but some might put up a stopping hand. Even the negative can provide us with vital information to keep going, take a detour, or maybe give a hard pass to that pursuit.

Even when we know we are headed in the right direction we can still face opposition and challenges. Again, we need to reach out to others for counsel, wisdom, and support.

Let's keep pedaling and remember to give ourselves permission to know that we need more help than we think we do: Make that phone call, meet with a friend, mentor, or counselor. Reach out to others. We aren't meant to pedal alone, and we must equip ourselves with the ways and people to make it through.

Above all else, know that God is smiling with every effort we make toward the dream. When we find ourselves overwhelmed by the task or journey at hand, remember the wisdom Neil offered that we can apply to any aspect of life. "How many pedal strokes across the country? Probably a million. Each pedal stroke matters. Little moments. I'm here in this second. I'm going to be present and get to the next one. I don't know what happens after that. I'm going to do this in this minute."[53]

Let's do everything we can to be present in the moment and take one more pedal stroke.

Chapter Eighteen

Braving the Unknown

I went skydiving for the first time a few years ago.

Before I even put on the flight suit, I watched a for-ty-five-minute video with explicit instructions on the activity. My jump instructor then walked me through what I learned in the video: the altitude we had to reach before jumping, how fast we would fall, and how to pay attention to the altimeter on my wrist.

At a specific point, I needed to reach down, grab, and pull the release to launch the parachute. There were specific ways to hold my hands, bend my legs, lift my head.

It was terribly unnerving, but my instructor, James, assured me that he would be attached to my jumpsuit in several places. I wore no helmet—his helmet was my helmet; his parachute was my parachute. I found myself completely dependent on him and his gear for safe passage and landing. Literally, I depended on him for my life.

He was there to ensure I did everything I learned in a timely, safe manner. As we rose higher and higher in the small, crowded, noisy plane, he casually asked if I wanted to play it safe or have a wild ride.

Having zero details about either choice, I opted for the wild ride (this included a flip out of the plane and lots of spins once the parachute opened).

As the plane rose higher, all I could think about was what I needed to do after we jumped and my instructor released the mini parachute to maintain our minute-long freefall rate of 120 miles per hour.

That is our life sometimes, isn't it? We don't even need to jump out of a plane to feel that feeling of freefall!

When we boarded the plane, we were unattached, and about 12,000 feet up he began attaching his jumpsuit carabiners to mine. After he clipped us together, I asked repeatedly if we were securely connected.

He assured me he was in control, that we were locked together, and as we scooted down the bench to the open doorway of the plane, I peppered him with questions. I'm certain he couldn't hear specifics over the engine and wind noise; he just kept smiling and giving me two thumbs up.

Before I could think twice and back out of this situation, I watched my nephew and his instructor jump out and begin their freefall ahead of us.

Then we were up, crouched in the open doorway of the plane.

I will never forget looking down into the empty atmosphere, watching my instructor's arm move with our signal . . .

One . . .

Two . . .

Threeeeeeeeee . . . and down we tumbled.

We fell, flipped, engaged the small safety chute to slow our speed a bit, watched the altimeter, pulled the parachute, and glided for a few minutes. (At a critical point, he even had to grab my wrist and show me the altimeter as a reminder that I needed to pull the parachute!) Our landing was fairly smooth as we bounced across the grass and came to a stop.

Wow! What a scary, awesome, fantastic, wonderful, exhilarating, crazy ride. I have one mid-air picture showing me with a huge smile on my face.

It was completely forced.

That high up, the power of the cold wind wouldn't allow me to breathe very well or close my mouth. During our instructions, I was told that I needed to remember to smile and look at the photographer who jumped out of the plane before us and captured it all on video. My forced face looked happy through my terror and inability to breathe.

Isn't that how our lives often feel?

Out of control, in a life freefall, wondering if we are securely attached to anything as we tumble into the upside-downs of our lives.

Where do we find our security?

When I think about my constant questioning up in that plane, making sure I was attached to my instructor, I think, "Oh my, am I ever that concerned with checking on my connection with Jesus?"

We prepare for the upside-downs of life by spending so much time abiding in him that winds may blow and storms may come through, but because of our experience, assurance, and testimony of his past work, we have access to the peace that passes all understanding at the very core of who we are, even in the midst of challenging times.

I am now passionate about upside-down pre-work.

If you are not a person of faith, where do you seek your confident connection? How do you prep for the winds of change or face exciting, unknown challenges?

The turning points came when I struggled through life events that didn't make sense. I questioned God. I was desperate to follow him but was suffering great confusion. Yet the years of those experiences drove me straight to him in search of understanding. I learned each time and became more strongly rooted in the reality of trusting him with every single step.

When the "What Ifs . . ." Flood Our Minds

I have a habit of playing a game. The "What If" game. Not the fun kind either.

It feels like I've spent much of my life energy thinking, "But, what if _____ happens (in a negative, catastrophic sense)?"

I'm an optimistic, outgoing, joy-seeking person, but this game seems to lurk just beneath the surface, waiting for those moments when I'm stressed or tired or insecure.

Do you ever find yourself thinking, "Yes, but, what if _____ happens?"

I've faced underlying and sometimes surface worry because I posed the negative form of "what if." The irony? What I worried about usually didn't happen, and I wasted time, energy, and opportunity.

Life normally unfolds in ways I never expect and therefore have no way to prepare.

Maintaining healthy balance offers a defining step to prep for the unknown. Is it smart to have emergency supplies and food for physical needs and to prepare our hearts and shore up our foundations for emotional and mental needs? Yes.

However, it is a balance and I want to move forward erring on the side of the positive.

I'm trying to reframe this and play a new game of "What If."

I still ask, "But, what if _____ happens," but I reframe the question toward the positive. Instead of pondering the negative possibilities, I turn my thoughts to anticipate positive possibilities that could happen.

When we rebuild, remodel, reframe our life, let's be wary of the negative—self-talk and old, unproductive remnants that play in our heads. Let's remember who we are and grab onto God-confidence, keep healthy boundaries in place, and not lead ourselves down the path of negativity.

Remember, strength comes with each brave step into the dark unknown.

Let's fully live one step at a time. Along the way we try, we learn, we gather our community in which we experience the give and take of encouragement, accountability, cheerleading, loving truth, and strong support.

When we face great winds of change, let's remember to stop, breathe, and evaluate the situation to the best of our ability.

Traumatic and confusing times can cause us to step back and question God, sometimes even raising our hurting voices to heaven. We can prepare in the peaceful times by abiding and remaining faithful in him.

We need to support and encourage each other in our earthly realities.

Let us not allow the upside-down times to completely take us out of this life game! Our preparation and obedience to abide in Christ requires daily action—focused, intentional, and mindful.

Trust me, I learned the hard way that I'd spent much of my life living with Jesus as my savior for eternity but not as Lord over the everyday details of my life. Now I do my best to keep turning back to him in everything and not compartmentalizing my faith and the rest of my life but incorporating all of it together.

Keeping Our Margin

In all of the busyness of life, with the demands of jobs, commitments, and family, how are we to guard time to walk with, help, mentor, and care for others, much less dream about possibilities for ourselves?

We must be careful to give ourselves enough margin.

My friend Melinda has worked in ministry for the majority of her adult life. During a conversation about leadership, she told me one of the most important things she has learned in her work and life in general is to leave margin for God, others, and life events.

She said life can get really busy, and we can fill our days with good things, often too many worthy things.

She explained her approach and gave me such a great visual:

"Picture a buffet or family-style dinner with many offerings of food. If I get a large dinner plate and go through the line sampling lots of things, pretty soon I don't have any unoccupied space left on the plate—there is no margin left. I think of my life like a dinner plate now. I pay attention to those things that I need to do and leave open space for those last-minute necessities: a friend who needs me, a conversation with someone desperate for an understanding ear, maybe an emergency situation where I can serve and care for someone. If my schedule is crammed full (my plate has no unoccupied space left), I have no margin for those every day, last-minute people and events that God might put in my path."

When she gave me this advice, I cringed. You see, at the time, I had just gone through an ordeal because of overcommitment. Along with graduate school classes, which gave me a ton of work, I was a lay speaker and teacher at church, on the board of a nonprofit in my community, and had committed to help form a women's ministry and chair its board at the church I attended.

Several weeks after I entered a new season of graduate work, I found I couldn't continue in the same way and serve anyone well. I might have managed to juggle all of them, but not effectively and not in a responsible way.

A longtime mentor listened and empathized as I honestly shared my overcommitment and came to the conclusion that school needed to have my focus. I sadly stepped back from my role with the nonprofit and met with teaching teams to say I couldn't participate for a while. The most difficult and emotional conversation came when I had to swallow my pride, call the three women who originally invited me to help form and lead the women's ministry board, and tell them I had to step down.

Even in the midst of making the decision that served everyone in a better way, I felt heartbroken, embarrassed, and ashamed about my shortsightedness and overcommitment.

When we leave margin in our lives, we can stay aware of where we spend much of our time. Technology and social media are good tools but can suck us dry, distract us from important actions, and keep us in a mindless state.

How often do we look at how we spend our time? Do we abide in our technology? The closeness, dedication, time spent, focus, addiction? When we arise in the morning, do we reach for our phones before we get out of bed?

Do we say something as simple as, "Good morning, God, thank you for a new day. Help me pay attention to what or who you put before me. Fill me with an awareness of your presence and help me live today as you would have me live." I realized recently that my time with the Lord was sadly lacking, but my attention to social media was habitual.

One of the best cases for margin lies in the additional space and freedom it gives us to nurture and care for nature and animals, which actually helps us at the same time.

Chapter Nineteen

Nurturing Life

*F*all is my favorite time of year. Growing up in Texas, I learned that this season has its limitations—it lasts a brief time, and the rich, saturated autumn colors don't really thrive. I love having opportunities to visit other places and take in the true fall hues.

Once I went to a plant show and found a shantung maple. The grower promised that he had developed this drought-tolerant, Texas-friendly maple that would produce the rich, orange-red leaves like trees in the northeastern part of the US. The grower promised it would reach twenty to thirty feet one day.

The saplings sat in ten-gallon plastic buckets. They looked like little Charlie Brown trees.

In my quest to have beautiful autumn color in my yard, I bought one. I took the scrawny tree home and set the plastic bucket out in a flowerbed, looking for the perfect location.

Unfortunately, a situation arose with backyard erosion and the flowerbed had to be removed, the fence rebuilt, and more. As often happens with remodel and construction, it took much longer than promised. The entire yard was torn up for several months.

One day, I walked around a corner and saw the forgotten bucket on its side. The tiny tree desperately needed a drink and space to root and grow. I found the appropriate spot and optimistically planted it. I had to set low expectations for its survival.

The only location in my yard acceptable for the anticipated height was in the direct west sun where the August days were mercilessly beating down on it. At one point the struggling tree even suffered from sun scalding, something I didn't even know existed.

Two years of regular watering, nutrients, and space in a safe environment aided this little tree in developing an incredible root system and a gorgeous canopy of limbs and leaves.

When trees and plants are well rooted, they gain what they need to flourish and grow.

The same happens with us.

When we abide with Christ, our spiritual roots grow and we gain abundant life in him. We learn more about who we are. When we give space *to* him, we discover extraordinary life *in* him.

As you go through your calendar and plan activities, make sure to leave margin for the unexpecteds that nurture you and also offer ways for you to reach out and care for others. Leaving space and time for reflection and growth will add to the beauty of your story.

Look at the story of you he unfolds
as he enfolds you day by day.

Nurturing Ourselves

As we've worked on knowing more about ourselves, determining who we want to be, how to make choices and space to walk in excellence, people to gather and practices to put in place, let's pause for a minute to talk about nurturing ourselves.

So often, we think self-care sounds selfish or self-serving, but we are our own advocates. Sure, we can skim through life, keeping up with daily responsibilities, tending to everyone else's needs, and meeting the demands of our jobs and homes. That can all work for a while.

But let me offer an additional layer.

During a recent conversation with a friend who knows all about my life, we talked about how we each have areas and layers that require nurturing. So often, no one outside of ourselves even knows about these depths.

As we grow, mature, and manage our lives, we tend to add more activities and responsibilities. At the same time, we push down those dreams, desires, and talents that are part of us.

We are each a unique creation of Almighty God, here for this time and place. He created you and me and gave us individual gifts, talents, and desires in our hearts. If we remain too busy or distracted, we might not pay attention and even miss out on joyful opportunities to use them or even know we have them.

Taking steps through margin and attention to develop a better understanding of our uniqueness helps us to encourage ourselves and invite others in to give support and input as well.

When we seek to nurture ourselves, our surroundings, and others, we give depth of meaning and joy to our lives and establish intentional interactions with all.

Intentional Interaction

Thirty-eight hours before my dad passed away, I stopped by my parents' house in a great hurry.

My dad was on hospice and had been sick for a long time, but nothing seemed imminent and this was just a quick in-and-out to see him.

He had pajamas on, sitting in a chair by the bedroom window. I sat down for a quick catch-up, visited a little while, then jumped up to leave. I leaned over to kiss his cheek and tell him I would see him in a couple of days.

As I turned to go, he gently reached up and put his hand on my arm and I turned back. He intentionally paused until he had my full attention, looked into my eyes, and said slowly and firmly, "I. Love. You." It was a meaningful moment but only on reflection did the full import register.

Thirty-eight hours later, my mom called to tell me my dad had unexpectedly passed on.

I've often thought about our last interaction and wondered if he sensed the short time he had left on Earth and wanted to make sure the last thing he communicated was how much he loved me. And he wanted to make sure I took it in.

How often does our Heavenly Father try to gently get our attention to say "I. Love. You." by giving us a constant sense of his presence, if only we would take the time to stop and draw near. For a moment . . . to witness a beautiful sunset over the water, before or during our capture of the photo, then give him silent or verbal thanks and praise.

Hearing treasured voices greeting us in our regular routine, do we say a silent prayer acknowledging our gratefulness to him for loved ones' presence in our lives? What about when we sense his love and encouragement through the voices and wisdom of friends?

May we remember and commit to intentional interactions with our loved ones and our God throughout our days.

Lighten Our Load

I recently came across a picture of myself leaning against a brick column in a foreign train station—not in a *looking-cool-hip-cosmopolitan-trendy-traveler-nonchalant* kind of lean but in a *desperately-seeking-support-for-this-way-too-heavy-bag-hanging-on-my-back* kind of lean.

My large canvas suitcase hung on my back between me and the lovely column. I can remember the moment a friend took the picture and the relief I felt to find a momentary spot to stand and let the column support my load for a bit.

That particular overseas trip was part business, part fun, and I was determined to carry it off with just a large carry-on. It had hidden backpack straps so I could hop on and off trains and in and out of taxis with ease. HA!

The challenge came when my overpacking self, overloaded the bag. Even though I tried to travel with only a carry-on "backpack," I didn't adjust the number of items included in the load. The recommended bag worked beautifully—it was the packer who failed miserably and had residual arm and back pain to prove it.

What emotional loads do we travel with in our lives? Do we drag around overstuffed bags or multiple bags that require a baggage cart? Walking forward into new possibilities seems hopeful and intimidating at the same time.

Let's make sure what we carry won't hinder our possibilities for the next season.

Step Out

Speaking of what we carry with us, what about the weight of our thoughts? We can't help what pops into our minds, but we can control how long it stays.

Fear of the unknown carries an oppressive heaviness with it. During times of uncertainty, what if we reframe it with our new positive *what if* consideration? *What if* the next step that seems scary leads to a lifelong impact for good in our lives or someone else's life? If we are too scared and focused on our fear, our doubts, and our insecurities, we sit paralyzed in our zone of the known.

When we step into the unknown, let's take a breath and fill our lungs and insides with strength and courage, then engage in that next momentum step that keeps nudging us forward.

If you need added inspiration, think about it this way: If you could impact one other person, give a glimmer of hope or change the direction for them, would you?

When has someone done that for you? How did it feel? What happened? What was the result? Have you told them what a difference they made in your life?

Now, consider reaching out to someone else to offer similar hope. Reach within yourself to gain ground toward shoring up your own brave steps and possibilities.

As an added bonus to stepping out with new decisions, hold on to childlike wonder. This summer, for the first time in a long while, I saw an abundance of fireflies, which took me right back to warm summer nights playing barefoot in the grassy backyard. What are favorite childhood snapshots of happy times for you?

When we mine our childhood wonder, especially the simple times that brought us inner joy, we can get back in touch with the mindset where everything is a new possibility. Even if only for a few minutes, we can close our eyes and momentarily escape from the realities of our challenges and remember the joy and wonder of discovery.

We can't live there, but we can rebuild that part of our thought process to enhance our ability to step out of our routine when necessary and dream of new possibilities to explore and adventure throughout our lives.

Dream with me for a few minutes.

What came to mind when you read the earlier question I like to ask people who gather around my table? What would you do in life if talent, skills, money, education, experience, and opportunity were not factors or roadblocks? If you could do anything, what would it be?

Now that we've thought a bit about our dreams, how do we begin to integrate new opportunities and dreams into our reality? Let's look at some key steps to take as we set a new vision for our journey. These will help keep us on track with more focus, hope, and courage!

Chapter Twenty

Gaining Momentum

*W*hen I see posts about routines, lifestyle, habits, or journaling, my gut instinct goes straight to stress. I'm not, and never have been, a very structured person.

Maybe you can relate, or maybe you are way more organized than I am. Wherever you find yourself on the spectrum of daily structure, be encouraged. My new approach lies first in giving myself permission to do what works for me. That frees me from unnecessary, overriding stress.

Choose different tools to use and people to listen to. Be creative and make your own personalized dailies to follow.

Several years ago, I found myself trying to implement everything suggested and posted by a well-known voice in leadership. I became overwhelmed trying to do it all. A while later, another popular speaker and author caught my attention. I thought theirs might be more doable, so I quickly signed up and jumped in.

This approach became a pattern and I started to feel like a failure. Then I realized many of these super-successful people have a team working in the background. I jumped in each time trying to establish my individual work and systems on a level with those who'd been building their team for a long time.

I had to make it all work for *me*. So now I approach experts with more mental space: utilizing an idea from this person, following that person, and soaking up their wisdom. We can't be clones of another. We can admire their work and bring into our world the systems that enhance what we do. Just be careful of the avalanche of information, how it impacts your mind and spirit, and how easily it springs the comparison trap.

While we seek information to improve ourselves and learn how to fulfill new opportunities we pursue, a few simple daily steps could become rituals of a life rhythm that keep us steady, secure, and grounded when the winds blow.

Firsts to Implement:

First action

When we wake up to the alarm clock on our phone, we increase the temptation to turn it off and then immediately check email and social media. We wake up wanting to check on "vital" headlines to make sure we didn't miss anything overnight. When we do this, our day begins with distraction and sidelining.

What if we went old-school and set an alarm clock (digital or analog) to wake us up from a night's sleep? That way, we reach over to turn it off and there is no other action to tempt us.

First thoughts and prayer

Before our feet hit the floor, say a little prayer. "Lord, I give you this day (personalize this)."

First pages

Spend time with a paper Bible (to avoid the digital temptation). Journal your thoughts, thankfulness, or aspirations for the day.

Quietly sit with a cup of coffee or tea, listening to outside sounds or stream calming music. Just *be* for a few minutes.

After a little while, *then* move on to the rest of your routine: exercise, communication (maybe make intentional, connecting phone calls to core people), a healthy meal, and online engagement (news, email, social posts). Set a timer in order to be intentional and avoid getting stuck in a scrolling cycle. Do all of this with purpose and with healthy boundaries in place.

If you have littles in your house, this might be a challenge. If you're married, talk to your spouse about helping each other make room for a bit of individual quiet space. If you are single with children and have limited alone time in your schedule, send up short prayers and thankful praise as you engage with your kids and daily life responsibilities. Stop for ten seconds to look out the window up at the sky and think about a favorite Bible verse to help start your day with a little bit of mental and spiritual calm.

Developing Rhythm for Abundant Steps

We find assurance in the general rhythm of days and seasons—the rising and setting of the sun, the new life of spring arising from the grey dormancy of winter.

Develop your own life rhythm to cultivate hope while living in the reality of a personal storm. Remind yourself of these seasonal rhythms, then add new, individual encouragement. Think to yourself, "I look forward to tomorrow with hopeful expectation. I will go do _____." Plan something even if it seems really simple:

- Rise early, get dressed, and go try a new coffee/tea place.
- Read a few pages of an inspirational book.
- Go visit a friend who has a new puppy.
- Call your bestie to go on a short nature walk.
- Go to a local art museum and just wander, taking in the calm quiet and beauty.

Let these or other minimal activities give you a time of easy life engagement and even a creative rest from your difficulties. If you feel intimidated to visit a museum, remember, we don't have to be art experts to appreciate the incredible talent and passion of someone who lived their own story of ups and downs long before we did and transformed their story into a beautiful work of art.

Develop a daily rhythm of thought. Adding curiosity into our thoughts will take up space the negativity tries to capture. When we get into the mental habit of thankful thoughts, even something as simple as, "I'm grateful for the birdsong early this morning," we push aside the comparison trying to camp out in our brain. The more positive and good we intentionally and mindfully put in, the less negativity and toxic subliminal thoughts are able to hide out in the corners, ready to spring into action and sound a reminder alert when we feel tired and vulnerable.

Be encouraged to stand firm in the winds and push through the fear of failing, of not being good enough, of not being worthy.

You are valuable and have great worth.

Don't be afraid to be vulnerable, human, imperfect.

When we move through our days with an attitude of gratitude, an interdependent mindset, and a solid commitment to who we want to be all day in every situation, we build up our confidence and enable surer steps. The more we implement these dailies and develop life momentum, the more foundational grounding we have for surprising events in our lives.

Just Give It Two Weeks

Early on in our time together, I mentioned new winds of change in my life that involved relocating to a place far from my hometown.

While I don't fully understand the complete picture of why I felt led for so long to explore living in this new location or why at this particular time in my life God unfolded events so incredibly that I couldn't say no, I seek to embrace the opportunities as much as possible. That said, in the middle of it all, I've had some real-life winds blowing.

Moving during what I'd hoped was the tail end of a pandemic (it wasn't) to a place where I only had a few acquaintances, at the beginning of summer (people are in and out of town and have inconsistent summer schedules), and during a season of friend and family celebration times (that I would miss) might not have been my wisest choice!

I'm a people person and big on community (could you tell yet?), and there was something really lonely about not having my people around for summer holidays or activities (although kind new friends have included and invited me to several events).

When we have "our person" to explore a new place with, or a job in an office with other people, or kids to provide a way to meet other parents, a move can still have challenges. However, when all three are absent, the all-by-myself pity party sure starts up with a vengeance!

My friend Lisa called one day to check on me as she had been doing since I moved. I felt the lonely feels that day and said, "Maybe I should come home." At the time of that phone call, a holiday was around the corner, I'd been in my new place for a couple of months, and I felt all the weight of loneliness hitting at once. I missed my friends, family, and church. She kindly listened and said, "Yes, you can come home."

Pause.

"Do you still feel like that is where God wants you even though you aren't entirely sure why yet?" (She asked in a curious, non-judgmental tone.)

"Yessss . . ." I drew out in answer.

"I get it. Reminds me of when I went off to college and called my dad sobbing. I told him, 'Listen, this isn't going to work. I can't stay here and I want to come home.'"

Her father's response? "Sug (short for sugar), can you give it two weeks? Just two weeks."

"Dad, I can't!" Sobbing with every syllable, Lisa repeated, "I just can't. This just isn't going to work out."

"Sug, just give it two weeks."

All these years later, Lisa remains truly thankful her dad encouraged her. I am too.

Her dad's request offers us a beautiful nugget of how to deal with new opportunities. There isn't much we can't do for two weeks. That offers a reasonable, bite-sized amount of time to consider trying something new.

I'm grateful for her sharing that story on a night when I needed sound advice presented in a loving "dad-like" way.

"Sug, just give it two weeks." I've repeated it to myself many times over the months I've been here.

Are you trying something new and feeling inadequate, uncertain, or lonely—but you know it is where you need to be right now?

"Sug, can you give it two weeks?"

When those two weeks pass and you've made it through, consider another two weeks. That amount of time is brilliant and really, for most things in life, we can handle something for two weeks. Then two more.

Lisa stayed and loved her college experience. I'm most grateful for her dad's advice because I arrived there her second year—fifty-two weeks later. We became friends, and our friendship has lasted a lifetime.

If you stand in a painful time or you're walking through a grief journey and your frame of reference falls into the "I'm not gonna make it here" or "this isn't going to work out" or "I don't know how I can get through this time" mentality, sometimes we have to focus on just getting through a much smaller amount of time and taking the next defining step.

How often in our dismay, debris, and lonely mindset do we think we can't make it through a particular day: Christmas, Thanksgiving, the anniversary of a sad or devastating event? I've gone through this for many reasons during different timeframes and here is what I've learned.

It feels overwhelming leading up to that month, week, day, or hour, and we need shoring up to summon the courage to meet it. If we have community close by, we call on someone to walk through the day with us. If not, or if we want to be alone, we get through that day remembering it is just one day.

Sug, you can do this for one day. And the next. And the next.

The point is we must readjust our mindset to meet the timeframe in a practical way so we aren't emotionally, mentally, or physically overwhelmed by despair.

Big holidays and celebration days are especially tough. Those holidays when advertisers and social media show "perfect" posts can make us feel like failures or "less thans" or place an emphasis on what we find missing in our lives. If we can process the pain a bit and look at it in the most basic way and reframe it in our head, we can break it down into a smaller amount that allows us to consider it as just another day.

Once we walk through that day, we realize it can be done. The world didn't stop spinning. All is okay. There might still be pain, but we made it through, and sometimes all we can do is One. Day. At. A. Time.

In no way am I dismissing your swirling emotions about a difficult day or event. Seriously, I've lived some of those dreaded times.

What I want to encourage here is for you to break it down into smaller, manageable pieces in your mind and really look at it differently for a little while in order to put it in its immediate place. A coping skill, if you will. And think in your head, whatever is right for you. "I can do this for another hour . . . or day . . . or week . . . or two weeks." Stay in the immediate timeframe and go no further into the future.

We want to be here, now. Be present in this day and grow stronger. We don't know what next week, month, or year will look like, so fretting about how we will face it only adds a burden of anxiety that we have no way to address. If you are a believer in Jesus, we learn that his grace meets us in our place of need the moment we step into that space.

To help my adjusting timeframe in a new place, I've also given myself permission and freedom to go home at any point I choose. That alone relieves tension and allows me to commit myself to continue the new adventure with flexibility. I've learned that the more people I meet, the more sights I see, and the more I learn about this new place, the better equipped I am to make an informed decision about whether or not I have found my long-term home.

I've had to adopt ways to have conversations with myself that I would typically have with a friend trying the same thing, reinforcing that it is okay to have lonely moments, that I'm not a loser for not having lifelong friends here, or understanding more about this city. Why would I? I'm brand new here.

The amount of pressure we can place on ourselves to be perfect or "look" like we have it all together can feel like such a burden, can't it?

But if all of us look like we have it all together at all times, what are we showing others about how to handle a crisis?

When we can authentically admit vulnerability or messed up moments, we can laugh together when necessary, find joy, and express empathy.

During a time of great vulnerability for me, as a result of an uplifting conversation with my cousin, Karen, I now regularly pray this prayer: "Lord, you have strategically placed me in this time and place. Empower me to do what you have for me, for the good of others, and for the glory of you alone."

Karen encourages me to walk forward with God-confidence as he has prepared and trained me, provided talent and skills, and seen me through past experiences. He has brought all things together for this time and place, and I must choose to draw assurance that these pieces put into place by him will come together and unfold for the next stage.

Finding Wisdom in Community

My other friends and relatives have offered ongoing advice and wisdom as well. My niece, Kristen, encouraged me to get a ticket to an event I was interested in but too insecure to go alone. She said, "Get a ticket and go! Your new best friends might be there just waiting to meet you!"

My new local friend, Karen, continues to encourage me by saying, "There's a town full of friends you just haven't met yet."

Suzanne said, "For the next three months, go and do things alone that you might not want to do. That isn't a long timeframe. Give it every chance and meet every opportunity; when you feel overwhelmed and alone, think of God being with you and being your buddy in the experience. Think of every hard thing you do as an act of worship and obedience in a place and time where you aren't sure what he has for you there. Obey, choose, and see everything as an act of worship for him."

From their mouths, through my typing, to your ears, I pray you will also find helpful action in their wisdom!

Chapter Twenty-One

Conclusion

One day, while talking to my mom, I mentioned that I'd been looking for a felt hat but couldn't find one I liked. At the time, I was packing bags for my move and trying to decide what clothes to take. Suddenly, she said, "You know I still have one of your dad's felt hats. You're welcome to it if you want it."

Well, I tried his hat on and loved it, so she kindly gave it to me. As I packed the car, I carefully placed the hat on top of a box. When I drove off toward my new adventure, I felt my dad's strength and my mom's love riding along with me.

When life uproots you and you start over or you decide you want to move somewhere new, grab hold of confidence, bravery, and kindness. Remind yourself you are a beloved, cherished child of God who is able. He is Almighty, Everlasting, Eternal, Creator, Sustainer of all.

Life might look different during times of uncertainty but keep striving and producing while staying flexible and alert to pivot in the delivery, if necessary.

You can accomplish great steps toward your dreams and passion, even when you don't realize that's exactly what is unfolding before you. This doesn't mean immersing yourself in needless busyness. In fact, focus on simplifying, putting down that which isn't yours to do anymore, and learn to dive deep into what you are called to do.

Limit distractions like mindless phone engagement and narrow down social media or other intake.

Feed your soul with meaningful words, books, Bible study.

Feed your eyes with enhancing visuals and stories, not just with the next binge-worthy show you hear about.

Stay willing and open. Pay attention to what God puts in front of you, noticing who crosses your path; who makes up the people connections in your life.

Determine where you are stuck. If necessary, recruit help. Explore ways you can gain momentum to take defining baby steps to move through and out from under the current burden that holds you down.

What are some theme words or key behaviors to define and remember? Write one to five words on the bathroom mirror or a Post-it Note (e.g., commit to be brave). What would it look like for you to be brave? What would the brave you choose or do?

Remind yourself to seek joy—it must be a daily choice.

Keep in the forefront of your eyes and mind the great value of your existence—God loves you. Write an inspirational quote or Bible verse to see and ponder on a regular basis.

So often, when we stand in the debris or fallout from an overwhelming situation, we need those who know us well to sit with us or talk to us and walk through what is at the heart of the "symptoms." Maybe even a counselor/therapist who is objective. We need others to help us think about life areas that might hinder true, vibrant, abundant living.

Often, we live in such a state of busy static that we no longer engage our senses to understand ourselves or our surroundings. Let's make a goal of growing our peace of mind. Take ten minutes once a week and go outside. Find a quiet, safe spot and sit with your eyes closed.

Ask:

- What sounds come alive? Really pay attention.
- What smells surround me in these few moments?
- How does this internal moment feel right now?

Now, open your eyes. What do you see right in front of you? Look closely. Make notes of all the different sights, sounds, smells, and textures you experience. Doing this regularly hones our senses and takes us to a place of keen awareness about ourselves and our surroundings.

As we work on our own times of rhythm, awareness, grace, and vibrant life, let's stay intentional about walking well with others too.

When a friend sits in the middle of their own situation of raw pain, or if someone expresses bitterness after a difficult time, wait a while to offer "encouragement" stories of God's care. We all have a different journey, and sometimes supporting looks like just sitting with them and actively listening.

We don't want to shame people if their experience plays out differently than ours. I know the tension can be great, and we can find ourselves wanting to jump in and fix everything for them and tell them how they should feel and what they should do.

This isn't our job—we want to love them well and, in doing so, we often don't need any words at all. Our presence speaks volumes.

God meets us when we step forward on our own journey or when we are invited to walk into sacred spaces of pain—his grace and kindness meet us in those moments.

Though the Winds Blow

Storms in life are inevitable, and yet somehow, I (maybe you too?) am usually surprised when they appear.

Out of nowhere.

The other day I stood outside and felt the wind pick up. I looked overhead and saw a dark mass of clouds swooping in.

The storm did not fit into my plan for the day.

You might recognize the scenario. Life feels good, giddy even, and then suddenly you look up. The sun shining on your oasis lies in the path of a menacing cloud ready to gobble it up.

The sky hangs a bit fuzzy with haze and the drops splashing on your face encourage a run for cover. Most of the time, these squalls throw harmless sounds around, nourish the ground, and then quickly move on.

Physical storms are bad enough. What do we do when the occasional emotional storm lashes our life, stays for an unwelcome amount of time, and leaves destruction in its path?

It made me think again about ways to act and respond.

Prepare

In a healthy, non-anxious way, we can prepare to the best of our ability. Many people have a stash of emergency supplies for bad weather and natural disasters—water, sturdy shoes, food, flashlights, batteries, first aid kit.

Just as we store supplies to meet basic physical needs, we can prepare for the emotional and spiritual storms of life.

- Having that personal support system in place: friends, family, neighbors. Knowing who we can lean on in times of need and offering the same support for them.
- Staying connected to a larger community: neighborhood, city, church, places where we are known and nurtured.
- Continually feeding ourselves positive messages: books, encouraging posts on social media, uplifting stories of other people who overcame challenges.
- Memorizing and holding inspiration inside: meaningful song lyrics, poems, quotes, and Scripture.

Pay Attention

Often a storm will appear without warning, but many times we are able to see signs if we pay attention. I don't mean living in fear or anxiety (these can be obstacles for me if I'm not careful) but living with intentionality and awareness.

- Life can overwhelm us with busy tasks and chaotic schedules. Push the pause button every few days and do a quick review of the different areas of life.
- Just stop and breathe.
- Notice who and what God places in our path.
- Look around and evaluate how events unfold. Spend quality time shoring up outer relationships and inner steadiness.
- Know and step into strengths and skills and invite friends to share what they see in us.

Hopeful Mornings

Sometimes we awaken to the sun offering bright optimism and hope, but issues still aren't working out the way we desire.

- Feel it, address it, and clear away debris.
- Invite people in who've been there.
- Assess damage and see the possibilities.
- Ask, "What do I have control over today?"
- Reach out and offer words of encouragement to ourselves and others.
- Cheer each other on! Be kind, grace-filled cheerleaders for other people.

Wispy Reminders

We began our time together talking about a literal, physical tornado and also the emotional storm of my divorce. No matter what we've been through (or will go through in the future), I want to issue this call to real talk for a moment.

No matter the preparation, choices, personal development, and positivity we gain in our lives, we *will* experience storms. If they are strong enough, they become part of how we are shaped over time. This reality doesn't need to make us feel hopeless. I want to be clear about the wispy shadow breezes in our memory bank that remain even as we take our defining steps forward in hope and courage.

After we walk through the rawness of grief, pain, or a devastating event, at some point, usually in a most unexpected way, we will have a jolt of remembrance.

Sometimes during a storm season, I can find myself unusually nervous about weather warnings and have to take a beat to have an internal chat or call someone else and talk through it.

I might hear a song, see the sun a certain way in the sky, or smell the great outdoors, and have a poignant moment of missing my dad.

In today's world of visuals and social media "memories," I occasionally feel startled when I see a post from several years ago that offers a difficult reminder of a challenging time.

Please don't let the jolts of remembrance overwhelm you with feelings of defeat. These wispy shadows don't need to take us down.

We can live in freedom from the burden of getting stuck under them by remembering all we've worked on and moved through with healthy, intentional steps. Pause to acknowledge the memory and resulting sadness or pain, and remind yourself that it is normal and understandable for the wisps to rise up on occasion. Then, keep doing the work for yourself, take a fresh hold on your faith, invite others into the struggle, and know you aren't alone in this experience.

Take the opportunity to transform the thought into something positive. When I have unexpected pangs of missing my dad, I remember how sick he was and tell myself I wouldn't want him to have to live like that again. Then I take an intentional moment to think about a joyful memory and say a prayer of thanks for the time I *did* have him here with me.

Press On

I never welcome storms. When they rage, I rely on my preparation and reach out to people who will encourage me to press on. Personal storms like death, illness, unfulfilled dreams, job loss, natural disasters, manmade disasters. These. Are. Tough. Times.

I try to remember that every bad situation or challenge provides an opportunity to grow, but I can't do it on my own.

We can't do life alone.

So, gather your peeps, your community, your grounding inspiration, your faith. Resolve to press on, press forward in life. There is a great reason for you, unique you, to be right where you are, to pour your beauty and talent into the world around you.

Though the winds of change blow and we experience life's unexpecteds, let's:

- Reframe negative thoughts.
- Build a firm foundation.
- Gather personal community.
- Put a positive twist on the what ifs.
- Steward our time and talent well.
- Live out our unique creation.
- Grab hold of our Wednesday.
- Pursue excellence in all we do.

Storms may come into our lives,
but they do not have the last word.
The sun will shine again.

In the introduction of this book, I posed several questions we would cover. As we close this part of our time together, how would you answer them now?

- Who are you as a uniquely created individual?
- What kind of person do you want to be?
- What is your desired destination? (How do you see it right now and stay flexible for future adjustments to the plan?)
- How do you find joy and hold onto contentment, compassion, and hope?

- In what ways can you engage with community, family, friends, co-workers, neighbors, and social media?

I know these questions aren't easily answered and it will take a while to fully work through them. Your answers might also change over time and be additionally shaped by future events. Come back to them again and again to gain clarity during new adventures and challenges.

Through it all, remember, it's a process.

I pray that through each new season you discover unique, wonderful truths about yourself and define your steps to craft an extraordinary life!

Irish Blessing

May you see God's light on the path ahead

When the road you walk is dark.

May you always hear, even in your hour of sorrow,

The gentle singing of the lark.

When times are hard may hardness

Never turn your heart to stone,

May you always remember when the shadows fall—

You do not walk alone.[54]

Acknowledgments

Thank you to my encouragers, accountability partners, mentors, and cheering friends and family who've walked me through extraordinary life events.

Les Carter, we've known each other for twenty-five years. Your wise counsel, mentoring, and coaching continue to enrich my life. You've helped me move through some challenging times and I'm grateful for your empathetic encouragement and assistance in developing clarity through a practical, grace-filled Christian lens.

Sue Edwards, you've been such a loving voice of guidance and friendship through some tricky (and joyful) times. Thank you for having my back, for offering prompts and biblical resolve, and, most of all, for your unconditional friendship and love. Your wisdom and calm in the midst of my most tumultuous years will never be forgotten, and I'm hopeful I can pass on the same to those coming along behind me.

Willie O. Peterson, you are a valued mentor, adviser, friend, and true brother in Christ. Thank you for engaging in my work and investing your time and energy to ask thoughtful questions and build my confidence, urging me forward into that which God has called me.

Many thanks to the entire team at Morgan James Publishing. I'm so grateful to work with all of you.

Karen Anderson, how blessed I am that God intersected our paths. I appreciate your friendship, encouragement, and heart for authors. You exuded great care while urging me to mold and shape my words. I am grateful for your friendship and coaching.

The *Bearing Life® Podcast* guests, thank you for sharing your stories that encourage and equip others to stand firm in hope and practical compassion.

Kelley Mathews, Sissi Haner, and Karen Hunsanger, my gratitude for each of you and your attention to the details and flow of these words.

Kyla, René, niece Kristen, and cousin Karen, each of you consistently offered extraordinary listening skills and beautiful wisdom over the course of many years. I treasure your friendship.

Jill, Clay, and Mom, I couldn't ask for more caring, supportive, and loving siblings and mother.

Dad, I'm grateful for the years I had with you, and the love, faith, and integrity you modeled for us all.

To my entire family, I love you and I'm so thankful you're mine!

About the Author

by Amelia J. Moore Photography

*J*ulie Shannon helps women reframe their story and navigate the unexpecteds in life with clarity, courage, and confidence.

Her experiences, relatable communication style, and generous personality create the perfect partner to encourage women's hearts, equip them with practical skills, and propel them to meaningful action.

Julie's professional background includes an undergraduate degree in Radio/TV Communication from Stephen F. Austin State University, a Master of Arts in Christian Education degree, and a Doctor of Educational Ministry degree from Dallas Theological Seminary.

She has twenty years of experience in speaking, teaching, and writing, which allows her message to resonate with her audience and inspire them in fresh new ways.

When she's not helping rally individuals and communities, you can find her on the alert for creative ideas and fun adventure. She adores music, writing, photography, nature, is an aspiring golfer, and loves spending time with friends, family, and her four-legged children.

Check out her two previously released titles: *When the Stork Passes By: A Field Guide to Practical Compassion* and *Infertility & Involuntary Childlessness: Traveling the Terrain.* You can also learn more about her, listen to episodes of her podcast, *The Bearing Life®*, or subscribe to her email updates at www.drjulieshannon.com.

SUBSCRIBE AND GET

the Winds of Change Companion Guide

drjulieshannon.com/thewindsofchange

Endnotes

1   Spielberg, Steven, director. *Indiana Jones and the Last Crusade*. Paramount Pictures, Lucasfilm, 1989.

2   Shannon, Julie. "Processing Trauma." *The Bearing Life®*. Podcast audio, September 15, 2021. https://drjulieshannon.com/processing-trauma/.

3   Shannon, "Processing Trauma."

4   van Der Kolk, Bessel. *The Body Keeps the Score*. New York, NY: Penguin Books, 2014.

5   Shannon, Julie. "Processing Trauma." *The Bearing Life®*. Podcast audio, September 15, 2021. https://drjulieshannon.com/processing-trauma/.

6   Shannon, "Processing Trauma."

7   Shannon, Julie. "Contentment in Singleness." *The Bearing Life®*. Podcast audio, February 10, 2021. https://drjulieshannon.com/contentment-in-singleness/.

8   Shannon, "Contentment in Singleness."

9   Shannon, "Contentment in Singleness."

10 Shannon, "Contentment in Singleness."

11 Ready, Keith. "The Nails in the Fence." *A Gift of Inspiration*, http://www.agiftofinspiration.com.au/stories/attitude/nails.shtml.

12 Shannon, Julie. "Contentment in Singleness." *The Bearing Life®*. Podcast audio, February 10, 2021. https://drjulieshannon.com/contentment-in-singleness/.

13 Shannon, "Contentment in Singleness."

14 Shannon, Julie. "Narcissism." *The Bearing Life®*. Podcast audio, March 3, 2021. https://drjulieshannon.com/narcissism/.

15 Shannon, "Narcissism."

16 Shannon, "Narcissism."

17 Shannon, "Narcissism."

18 Shannon, Julie. "Anxiety." *The Bearing Life®*. Podcast audio, October 28, 2020. https://drjulieshannon.com/anxiety/.

19 Shannon, "Anxiety."

20 Shannon, "Anxiety."

21 Ducharme, Jamie. "Depression Has Skyrocketed During the COVID-19 Pandemic, Study Says. *Time*, September 4, 2020. https://time.com/5886228/depression-covid-19-pandemic/.

22 Shannon, Julie. "Living with Depression." *The Bearing Life®*. Podcast audio, July 8, 2020. https://drjulieshannon.com/living-with-depression/.

23 Park, Alice. "Simone Biles Has the Twisties. What Are They, and Why Are They So Dangerous?" *Time*, July 30, 2021. https://time.com/6085776/simone-biles-twisties-gymnastics/.

24 Park, "Simone Biles Has the Twisties."

25 Shannon, Julie. "Family Legacy." *The Bearing Life®*. Podcast audio, February 24, 2021. https://drjulieshannon.com/family-legacy/.

26 Shannon, Julie. "Single Seasons." *The Bearing Life®*. Podcast audio, August 12, 2020. https://drjulieshannon.com/single-seasons/.

27 Shannon, "Single Seasons."

28 Shannon, Julie. "Mental Health." *The Bearing Life®*. Podcast audio, August 26, 2020. https://drjulieshannon.com/mental-health/.

29 Shannon, "Mental Health."

30 Shannon, "Mental Health."

31 Shannon, "Mental Health."

32 Shannon, Julie. "Purpose Through Disability." *The Bearing Life®*. Podcast audio, September 29, 2021. https://drjulieshannon.com/purpose-through-disability/.

33 Shannon, "Purpose Through Disability."

34 Shannon, "Purpose Through Disability."

35 Shannon, Julie. "Life Storms with Taurus, Part One." *The Bearing Life®*. Podcast audio, June 24, 2020. https://drjulieshannon.com/life-storms-with-taurus-part-one/.

36 Shannon, "Life Storms with Taurus, Part One."

37 Shannon, "Life Storms with Taurus, Part One."

38 Yates, David, director. *Harry Potter and the Order of the Phoenix*. Warner Bros., 2007.

39 Shannon, Julie. "Joy & Grief of Special Needs." *The Bearing Life®*. Podcast audio, October 7, 2020. https://drjulieshannon.com/joy-and-grief-of-special-needs/.

40 Shannon, "Joy & Grief of Special Needs."

41 Shannon, "Joy & Grief of Special Needs."

42 Shannon, "Joy & Grief of Special Needs."

43 Shannon, "Joy & Grief of Special Needs."

44 Shannon, Julie. "Bearing Grief, Part 1." *The Bearing Life®*. Podcast audio, July 22, 2020. https://drjulieshannon.com/ bearing-grief-part-1/.

45 Shannon, "Bearing Grief, Part 1."

46 Shannon, "Bearing Grief, Part 1."

47 *Superstar*. Season 1, episode 3, "John Ritter." Aired August 25, 2021, ABC.

48 Cunningham, Debbie. Music, "Fly." Accessed September 21, 2021. https://debbiecunningham.net/music.

49 Cunningham, Debbie. *Dancing in the Kitchen: Hope and Help for Staying in Love*. Audiobook. Accessed September 21, 2021. https://debbiecunningham.net/book-audio-book.

50 Cunningham, Debbie. "Transitioning Your Career—How I Went From Jazz Artist to Writer." Ms. Career Girl, April 1, 2019. https://www.mscareergirl.com/transitioning-your-career-how-i-went-from-jazz-artist-to-writer.

51 Shannon, Julie. "Big Dreams." *The Bearing Life®*. Podcast audio, October 6, 2021. https://drjulieshannon.com/big-dreams/.

52 Tomba, Neil. *The Listening Road: One Man's Journey Across America to Start Conversations About God*. Nashville, TN: Nelson Books, 2021.

53 Shannon, Julie. "Big Dreams." *The Bearing Life®*. Podcast audio, October 6, 2021. https://drjulieshannon.com/big-dreams/.

54 IrishCentral.com. "An Irish Blessing for Comfort in Times of Grief." Facebook post, October 2, 2017. https://www.facebook.com/IrishCentral/videos/10159372972725048.

A free ebook edition is available with the purchase of this book.

To claim your free ebook edition:

1. Visit MorganJamesBOGO.com
2. Sign your name CLEARLY in the space
3. Complete the form and submit a photo of the entire copyright page
4. You or your friend can download the ebook to your preferred device

Morgan James BOGO™

A **FREE** ebook edition is available for you or a friend with the purchase of this print book.

CLEARLY SIGN YOUR NAME ABOVE

Instructions to claim your free ebook edition:
1. Visit MorganJamesBOGO.com
2. Sign your name CLEARLY in the space above
3. Complete the form and submit a photo of this entire page
4. You or your friend can download the ebook to your preferred device

Print & Digital Together Forever.

Snap a photo

Free ebook

Read anywhere